The Biblical
Path
of Life

Year One ♦ Quarter Two

© 2019 M.J. Ross
All Rights Reserved

Editorial Design and book cover by **Sergio León**

Permission to copy the Q&A Sections granted
with purchase of this book.

Visit **www.biblicalpath.com** for additional lesson support,
and corresponding activity pages for children.

M.J. Ross

The Biblical Path of Life

Year One Quarter Two

In order to understand how to live a Christian life pleasing to God, one must first know what His Word says.

Shew me thy ways, O LORD;
teach me thy paths.

—Psalm 25:4

The Bible specifically reveals what God expects from His people, but most find it difficult to read and understand what the Bible says. The Biblical Path of Life is meant to simplify that process. It is a study to help anyone understand how simply the Bible is put together. This will make it not only interesting but applicable to everyday life. The study begins in the Old Testament, learning the foundational truths God showed His people from the beginning of time, but consistently refers to the familiar truths found in the New Testament. The principles of the Bible must be applied to Christians' lives in order for them to become more like Christ. This study can be for an individual, a family, a small-group Bible study, or even a Sunday School program for all ages.

All scripture quotations in this book are taken from the King James Version of the Bible.

PREFACE

God's Word is the most important thing we can know and teach. In order to understand how to live a Christian life pleasing to God, we must first know what His Word says. This study is meant to help anyone understand how simply yet intricately the Bible is put together. When we understand how the Bible fits together, we can understand it much easier.

In this study, we will take three years to go completely through the Bible. We begin with an overview of the 5 Old Testament Divisions. Next, we will study each section, remembering many familiar Bible events (and learning a few new ones along the way). The idea is to see the Bible in historical order to alleviate some of the confusion. For the first two years, at the end of each quarter (every thirteenth lesson), we will take out time to see Jesus in the Old Testament.

This study was put together to make the Bible not only interesting, but also applicable to everyday life. The Bible means nothing to us if we do not apply the principles within it to our lives to become more like Christ.

At the end of some sections is a section called "A Deeper Path." This offers more information to help readers to think deeper if they are already familiar with some of the Bible events. Sometimes the Bible has more to say about certain subjects. These additions are to help readers consider what else the Bible may reveal about the people and events as they are studied.

YEAR ONE - 1st. Quarter

Overview of Old Testament
(Old Testament and Five Divisions):

Lesson 1 The Seven Dispensations

Lesson 2 God Made Me

Lesson 3 Why Is the History Important?

Lesson 4 Thirty-Nine Old Testament Books: Five Divisions

Lesson 5 Five Books of the Law: Genesis to Deuteronomy

Lesson 6 Twelve Historical Books: Joshua to Esther

Lesson 7 Five Personal Books: Job to Song of Solomon

Lesson 8 Seventeen Prophetic Books: Isaiah to Malachi

Lesson 9 Five Major Prophets: Isaiah to Daniel

Lesson 10 Nine Pre-exile Minor Prophets: Hosea to Zephaniah

Lesson 11 Three Post-exile Minor Prophets: Haggai to Malachi

Lesson 12 Review Old Testament Divisions

Lesson 13 Jesus in the Old Testament: **How Jesus Relates to the Old Testament**

YEAR ONE - 2nd. Quarter

Current Book

Five Books of the Law:
Genesis (Book of Beginnings);
Exodus (Book of Redemption);
Leviticus (Book of Worship);
Numbers (Book of Wanderings);
Deuteronomy (Renewed Covenant)

Lesson 1	Genesis 1–11: Four Main Events: Creation, Fall, Flood, Babel	28
Lesson 2	Genesis 12–24: Abraham and Isaac	44
Lesson 3	Genesis 25–36: Jacob	62
Lesson 4	Genesis 37–50: Joseph	86
Lesson 5	Exodus 1–18: From Egypt through the Wilderness	110
Lesson 6	Exodus 19–40: God Revealed	130
Lesson 7	Leviticus 1–20: The Way to God	152
Lesson 8	Leviticus 21–27: The Worship of God	170
Lesson 9	Numbers 1–19: Wandering in the Wilderness	188
Lesson 10	Numbers 20–36: The Next Generation	208
Lesson 11	Deuteronomy 1–11: Remembering the Past and Reviewing God's Laws	232
Lesson 12	Deuteronomy 12–34: Planning the Trip into the Promised Land	248
Lesson 13	Jesus in the Old Testament: *Jesus Fulfilled the Law*	262

THESE THIRTEEN LESSONS ARE CONTAINED INSIDE THIS BOOK

INTRODUCTION **11** THE BIBLICAL PATH OF LIFE

YEAR ONE - 3rd. Quarter

First Five Historical books:
When Canaan Was Occupied before Exile:

Joshua (Conquest);

Judges (Disobedience);

Ruth (Righteousness during Judges);

1 Samuel (Transition to Monarchy);

2 Samuel (David's Rule) **and Begin 1 Kings**

Lesson 1 Joshua 1–11: Conquering the Land

Lesson 2 Joshua 12–24: Possessing the Land

Lesson 3 Judges 1–12: The Decline of the Judges

Lesson 4 Judges 13–21: The Tragedy of No King

Lesson 5 Ruth: A Picture of Redemption

Lesson 6 1 Samuel 1–7: Eli to Samuel

Lesson 7 1 Samuel 8–15: Saul

Lesson 8 1 Samuel 16–31: David Coming to the Kingdom

Lesson 9 2 Samuel 1–5: David Crowned as King

Lesson 10 2 Samuel 6–10: David the Conqueror

Lesson 11 2 Samuel 11–24: The Result of Sin

Lesson 12 1 Kings 1–11: David's Death and Solomon King

Lesson 13 Jesus in the Old Testament: **Jesus, Our Ruler**

YEAR ONE - 4th. Quarter

Five Personal Books:

Job (Righteous Man);

Psalms (Songs—Hymns);

Proverbs (Wisdom);

Ecclesiastes (the Preacher);

Song of Solomon (Love in Marriage)

Lesson 1 Job: The Test

Lesson 2 Psalms 1–41: Book 1

Lesson 3 Psalms 42–72: Book 2

Lesson 4 Psalms 73–89: Book 3

Lesson 5 Psalms 90–106: Book 4

Lesson 6 Psalms 107–150: Book 5

Lesson 7 Proverbs 1–9: Wisdom Is to Be Found Early

Lesson 8 Proverbs 10–24: Wisdom Is Necessary

Lesson 9 Proverbs 25–31: Wisdom Revealed

Lesson 10 Ecclesiastes 1–8: The Vanity of Man

Lesson 11 Ecclesiastes 9–12: The Conclusion of the Matter

Lesson 12 Song of Solomon: The Perfect Love

Lesson 13 Jesus in the Old Testament: **Jesus, Our Friend**

YEAR TWO - 1st. Quarter

Next 2 historical books:

The kingdom was divided – including their prophets.
Pre-exile:

I Kings 12 - 22 (Divided Kingdom),

II Kings (Carried away as captives),

* **Hosea** (love of God in spite of spiritual adultery),

* **Amos** (a prophet from the country),

* **Obadiah** (warning to those who persecute Israelites),

* **Jonah** (an unwilling/ reluctant prophet),

* **Nahum** (Prophesied the destruction of Nineveh).

Israel (the Northern Kingdom)

Lesson 1 I Kings 12-15: Rehoboam, Jeroboam, & Divided Kingdom

Lesson 2 I Kings 16:29- 22:53: Ahab & Elijah

Lesson 3 II Kings 1 - 2: Elijah & Elisha

Lesson 4 II Kings 3 - 9:10: Elisha

Lesson 5 II Kings 9:11 – 13:9: Jehu – Jehoahaz

Lesson 6 Jonah: The Reluctant Prophet

Lesson 7   Amos: The Prophet from the Country
Lesson 8   II Kings 13:9 – 15:15: Jehoash – Shallum: Wickedness Punished
Lesson 9   Hosea: God's Enduring Love
Lesson 10 II Kings 15:14-31; & 16 – 17: Shallum – Hoshea
Lesson 11 Nahum: Nineveh's Destruction Foretold
Lesson 12 Obadiah: Edomites' Destruction Foretold
Lesson 13 Jesus in the Old Testament: **Why Israel Needed Jesus**

* *Pre-exile Prophets*

INTRODUCTION 15 THE BIBLICAL PATH OF LIFE

YEAR TWO - 2nd. Quarter

Judah: Part 1:

Next 4 historical books when the kingdom was divided –
including their prophet:
Pre-exile:

I Kings (Divided Kingdom),

II Kings (Carried away as captives),

I Chronicles (Spiritual perspective of kingdoms)

II Chronicles (Spiritual perspective of downfall) – beginning
with the genealogy of the nation Israel and then following Judah
through the time of the kings, and

* **Joel** (plague of locusts).

Judah (the Southern Kingdom):

Lesson 1 I Chronicles 1-2: Adam – Genealogy of Judah
Lesson 2 I Chronicles 3 – 10: The Beginnings of the Kings – Saul
Lesson 3 I Chronicles 11 – 20: David Becomes King
Lesson 4 I Chronicles 21 – 29: David
Lesson 5 II Chronicles 1-9: Solomon and the Temple

THE BIBLICAL PATH OF LIFE 16 INTRODUCTION

Lesson 6	I Kings 12:1-15:24; II Chronicles 10 – 16: Rehoboam, Abijah & Asa
Lesson 7	I Kings 22; II Kings 3; II Chronicles 17 – 20: Jehoshaphat
Lesson 8	II Kings 8:16- 9; II Chronicles 21-22:9: Jehoram, Ahaziah
Lesson 9	II Kings 11-12; II Chronicles 22:10 – 24: Athaliah, & Joash
Lesson 10	Joel: A Message in a Plague of Locusts
Lesson 11	II Kings 14-16; II Chronicles 25 – 28: Amaziah, Uzziah, Jotham, Ahaz
Lesson 12	II Kings 18-20; II Chronicles 29 – 32: Hezekiah
Lesson 13	Jesus in the Old Testament: **The Last Adam**

* *Pre-exile Prophet*

YEAR TWO - 3rd. Quarter

Judah: Part 2:

Historical books when the kingdom was divided – including their prophets:
Pre-exile:

II Kings (Carried away as captives),

II Chronicles (Spiritual perspective of downfall) – beginning with the genealogy of the nation Israel and then following Judah through the time of the kings.

* **Isaiah** (foretold of Babylonian conquest & Suffering Savior),
* **Jeremiah** (Weeping Prophet – foretold of "Branch" of David),
* **Lamentations** (Poem – by Jeremiah – of the Fall of Jerusalem),
* **Micah** (Prophet to both kingdoms calling for people to "hear"),
* **Habakkuk** (Asked God why – God answered),

* **Zephaniah** (God's judgment and mercy).

Lesson 1 Isaiah: The Lord Saves
Lesson 2 Isaiah 1-39: A Picture of the Old Testament
Lesson 3 Isaiah 40-66: A Picture of the New Testament
Lesson 4 Micah: Hear God's Words
Lesson 5 II Kings 21; II Chronicles 33: Manasseh and Amon
Lesson 6 Zephaniah: God's Judgment & Mercy
Lesson 7 II Kings 22 – 23:30; II Chronicles 34-35: Josiah
Lesson 8 Habakkuk: He asked God Why & Was Answered
Lesson 9 II Kings 23:31–25; II Chronicles 36: Jehoahaz, Jehoiakim, Jehoiachin & Zedekiah (carried captive)
Lesson 10 Jeremiah, God's Prophet
Lesson 11 Jeremiah, God's Suffering Servant
Lesson 12 Lamentations
Lesson 13 Jesus in the Old Testament: **Jesus and the Cross**

* *Pre-exile Prophets*

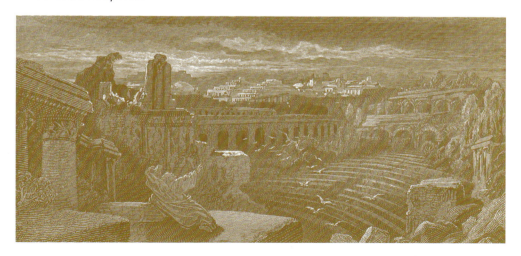

INTRODUCTION 19 THE BIBLICAL PATH OF LIFE

YEAR TWO - 4th. Quarter

Last 3 historical books, including their prophets
Post-exile:

* **Ezekiel** (foretold of "Shepherd" King),

* **Daniel** (foretold Messiah to be "cut off"),

** **Haggai** (God comes first),

** **Zechariah** (Finish – God's not finished with them yet),

** **Malachi** (last call before 400 year silence)

Lesson 1 Ezekiel 1-32: Judah's Fall

Lesson 2 Ezekiel 33-48: Judah's Future

Lesson 3 Daniel 1-4: Nebuchadnezzar, King of Babylon

Lesson 4 Daniel 5-12: Daniel, God's Man

Lesson 5 Ezra 1-5 & Haggai: Zerubbabel Begins Rebuilding the Temple

Lesson 6 Zechariah & Ezra 6: God's Plans for the Future
& the Temple Completed

Lesson 7 Esther: A Woman Who Saved her People

Lesson 8 Ezra 7-10: Ezra Restores the Relationship

Lesson 9 Nehemiah 1-6: Rebuilding the Walls

Lesson 10 Nehemiah 7-13: Instructions for the People

THE BIBLICAL PATH OF LIFE **20** INTRODUCTION

Lesson 11 Malachi: The Last Warning
Lesson 12 Jesus in the Old Testament: **The Promised One and His Messenger**
Lesson 13 Remembering the Old Testament

* *During Exile Prophets*
** *Post-exile Prophets*

INTRODUCTION 21 THE BIBLICAL PATH OF LIFE

YEAR THREE - 1st. Quarter

The Silent Years, an overview of the New Testament And the 4 Gospels:

- **Matthew**

- **Mark**

- **Luke**

- **John**

Lesson 1 400 Years of Silence & an Overview of the New Testament

Lesson 2 Jesus Birth & Childhood: The Four Gospels

Lesson 3 John the Baptist Introduces Jesus: The Four Gospels

Lesson 4 Jesus' Disciples: The Four Gospels

Lesson 5 Jesus' Miracles: The Four Gospels

Lesson 6 Jesus' Parables: The Four Gospels

Lesson 7 Jesus' Teachings: The Four Gospels

Lesson 8 Jesus' Personal Encounters: The Four Gospels

Lesson 9 Jesus' Final Journey: The Four Gospels

Lesson 10 Jesus' Death, Burial, and Resurrection: The Four Gospels

Lesson 11 Jesus is Alive: The Four Gospels

Lesson 12 Matthew & Mark: The King, yet a Servant

Lesson 13 Luke & John: A Man, but God's Son

THE BIBLICAL PATH OF LIFE **22** INTRODUCTION

YEAR THREE - 2nd. Quarter

The 2nd Division of the New Testament: The History Book:

Acts

Lesson 1 Power to be Witnesses: Acts 1 – 2

Lesson 2 Peter: Acts 3 – 5

Lesson 3 Stephen: Acts 6 – 7

Lesson 4 Philip: Acts 8

Lesson 5 Saul Becomes Paul: Acts 9:1-31

Lesson 6 Gentile Believers: Acts 9:32 – 11:18

Lesson 7 The Gospel Message Spreads: Acts 11:19 – 12

Lesson 8 Paul's First Missionary Journey: Acts 13 – 15:35

Lesson 9 Paul's Second Missionary Journey: Acts 15:36 – 18:22

Lesson 10 Paul's Third Missionary Journey: Acts 18:23 – 21:26

Lesson 11 Paul Arrested: Acts 21:27 – 23

Lesson 12 Paul Before Rulers: Acts 24 - 26

Lesson 13 Paul Shipwrecked: Acts 27 – 28

YEAR THREE - 3rd. Quarter

9 Epistles to churches:

Romans, I Corinthians, II Corinthians, Galatians, Ephesians, Philippians, Colossians, I Thessalonians, II Thessalonians

Lesson 1 How to get Saved: Romans 1 - 6

Lesson 2 How to Live Like You are Saved: Romans 7 – 16

Lesson 3 Following Christ: I Corinthians 1 - 6

Lesson 4 Stand Fast: I Corinthians 7 – 16

Lesson 5 Be Faithful to Christ: II Corinthians 1 – 5

Lesson 6 Growing in Christ: II Corinthians 6 – 13

Lesson 7 Learn to Walk in the Spirit: Galatians

Lesson 8 Faithful Saints in Christ Jesus: Ephesians

Lesson 9 Having the Mind of Christ: Philippians

Lesson 10 Keeping Christ as the Head: Colossians

Lesson 11 Possessing the Vessel in Sanctification and Honor: I Thessalonians

Lesson 12 Work Until Jesus Comes: II Thessalonians

Lesson 13 Review 3rd Division of the New Testament: Romans – II Thessalonians

YEAR THREE - 4th. Quarter

4 Epistles to Preachers, & 9 General Epistles:

I Timothy, II Timothy, Titus, Philemon, Hebrews, James, I Peter, II Peter, I John, II John, III John, Jude, and Revelation.

Lesson 1 I Timothy: Fight the Good Fight

Lesson 2 II Timothy: Be Faithful

Lesson 3 Titus & Philemon: Maintain Christian Living

Lesson 4 Hebrews 1 – 7: Jesus, our High Priest

Lesson 5 Hebrews 8 – 13: The Shadow Revealed

Lesson 6 James: Christians Show Faith by Works

Lesson 7 I Peter: Become Lively Stones

Lesson 8 II Peter: Growing in Grace

Lesson 9 I John: The Test of Faith: Truth vs. False

Lesson 10 II John, III John: Truth in Christian Living

Lesson 11 Jude: The Abandonment of God's Truth Revealed

Lesson 12 Revelation: The Revealing by Jesus Christ

Lesson 13 Review of the New Testament: Matthew – Revelation

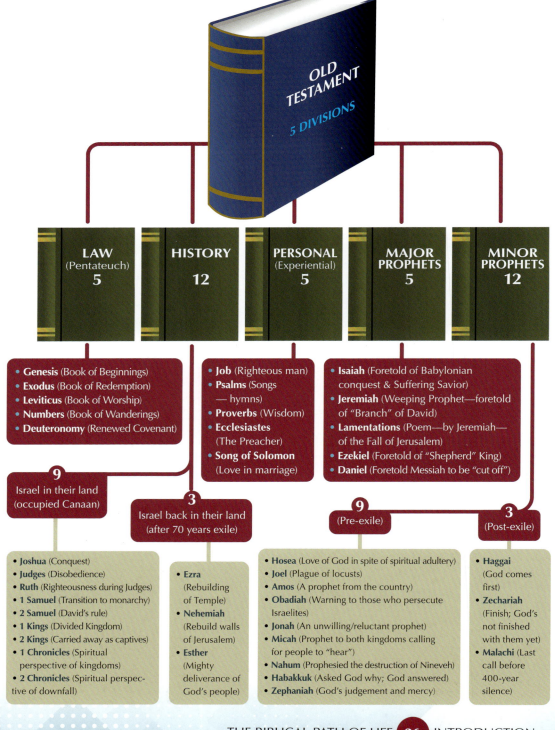

Old Testament Bookshelf

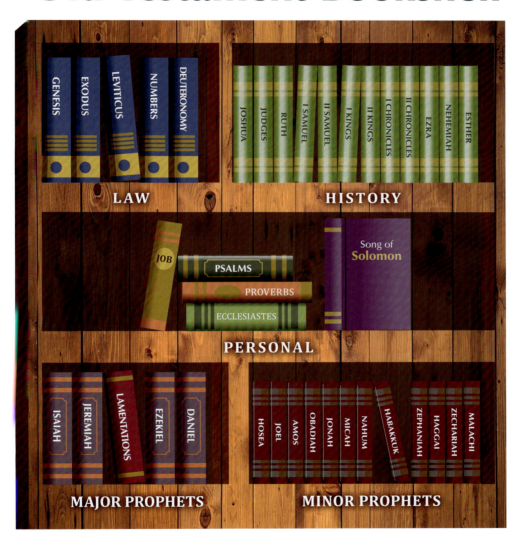

GENESIS 1–11:
FOUR MAIN EVENTS
CREATION, FALL, FLOOD, BABEL

LESSON 1

Key Verse

Trust in the LORD with all thine heart; and lean not unto thine own understanding.

— PROVERBS 3:5

Key Verse Thought: Read today's key verse. Understand that because we are humans, we cannot understand the things of God. We must learn to trust Him with all of our hearts.

Emphasis: We may not understand the things of God, but we are to rely upon God, not on our own understanding. We must learn to trust in the Lord with all our hearts and lean not to our understanding.

Lesson Summary: The events we will study today are mainly things we cannot really understand. That is why we must rely upon God and not our own

THE BIBLICAL PATH OF LIFE 28 LESSON 1

understanding (today's key verse). God created everything out of nothing. That is amazing, if you think about it. Who can understand how that is possible? God gave mankind everything they would ever need inside the garden. He asked only one thing—not to eat the fruit of one particular tree in the garden (Genesis 2:15–17). But that is exactly what Adam and Eve did. They disobeyed God and ate that one fruit. They didn't trust God's Word but leaned on their own understanding. When Eve saw that the tree was good for food, that it was pleasant to the eyes, and that it was a tree to be desired to make one wise, she took the fruit and ate it (Genesis 3:6). She tried to understand. She didn't trust God's Word.

By the time you get to Genesis 6, mankind had become exceedingly wicked—so wicked that God wanted to destroy all of His creation. "But Noah found grace in the eyes of the Lord" (Genesis 6:8). God spared Noah and his family. But by Genesis 11, the people had once again decided to choose what they wanted over what God told them to do. God had told the people to go forth and to fill the earth, but they came together and built a city and a tower to the heavens to make a name for themselves. Once again, God intervened in man's affairs.

Suggested Bible Reading to Prepare for This Lesson

- Monday: **Genesis 1–2**
- Tuesday: **Genesis 3–4**
- Wednesday: **Genesis 5–6**
- Thursday: **Genesis 7–8**
- Friday: **Genesis 9–10**
- Saturday: **Genesis 11**

Genesis 1–11: Four Main Events
Creation, Fall, Flood, Babel

1 Creation

- Genesis 1–2. All things created in six days, and on the seventh day, God rested
- Colossians 1:16–17

2 The Fall

- Genesis 3. Man disobeyed God's command—the fall of humankind from God's grace
- Romans 5:12

3 The Flood

- Genesis 6–9:19. God destroyed wicked mankind with a flood
- Genesis 6:8. Noah found grace in God's eyes
- 2 Peter 2:5
- Hebrews 11: 7
- 1 Peter 3:20

4. The Tower of Babel

- Genesis 11:1–9
- John 5:44
- Acts 2:4–8, 11–12

SPECIAL NOTE

We have now completed thirteen lessons for an overview of the Old Testament. In order to understand the Old Testament, we will study it in historical order, beginning with the books of the Law.

1. Creation

Genesis begins with creation. God created everything out of *nothing*. Who can understand how that is possible? (John 1:1–3; Ephesians 3:9). God gave mankind everything they would ever need inside the garden.

Genesis 1–2: All things were created in six days, and on the seventh day, God rested. (If you are teaching children, you may want to emphasize what was created on each day.)

- Day one: light divided from darkness (Genesis 1:3–5)
- Day two: separated the waters; made the heavens (Genesis 1:6–8)
- Day three: dry land separated from the waters; created all plants (Genesis 1:9–13)
- Day four: sun (to rule the day), moon (to rule the night) and stars (Genesis 1:14–19)
- Day five: all sea life and fowls of the air (Genesis 1:20–23)
- Day six: all of the animals that live on land, and man (Genesis 1:24–31)

The crowning glory of his creation was man, which He created in His own image. "26. And God said, Let us make man in our image, after our likeness: and let them have dominion over the fish of the sea, and over the fowl of the air, and over the cattle, and over all the earth, and over every creeping thing that creepeth upon the earth. 27. So God created man in his *own* image, in the image of God created he him; male and female created he them" (Genesis 1:26–27).

THE BIBLICAL PATH OF LIFE **32** LESSON 1

Remember, man was created without sin—sinless, just like God. God created man in righteousness and holiness. "According as he hath chosen us in him before the foundation of the world, that we should be holy and without blame before him in love" (Ephesians 1:4). God talked with man in the garden. "And they heard the voice of the LORD God walking in the garden in the cool of the day..." (Genesis 3:8a). God met with man to fellowship with him.

"16. For by him were all things created, that are in heaven, and that are in earth, visible and invisible, whether they be thrones, or dominions, or principalities, or powers: all things were created by him, and for him: 17. And he is before all things, and by him all things consist" (Colossians 1:16–17).

God created everything out of nothing.

LESSON 1 33 THE BIBLICAL PATH OF LIFE

2. The Fall

Adam and Eve expelled from Paradise.

While living in the garden and tending it, God asked only one thing of Adam and Eve—not to eat the fruit of one particular tree (Genesis 2:15–17). What did Adam and Eve do? They disobeyed God and ate that one fruit. They didn't trust God's Word. Satan came to Eve under the guise of a serpent, and he challenged God's Word as he spoke to Eve. She didn't trust God's Word. When Eve saw that the tree was good for food, that it was pleasant to the eyes, and that it was a tree to be desired to make one wise, she took the fruit and ate it (Genesis 3:6). Then Adam too ate the fruit. After thinking about it, they leaned on their own understanding. By their own reasoning, they chose to disobey God.

Genesis 3—Man sinned against God (The Fall).

"Wherefore, as by one man sin entered into the world, and death by sin; and so death passed upon all men, for that all have sinned" (Romans 5:12).

But don't forget God's promise. "And I will put enmity between thee and the woman, and between thy seed and her seed; it shall bruise thy head, and thou shalt bruise his heel" (Genesis 3:15). This is a promise of Jesus.

THE BIBLICAL PATH OF LIFE   34   LESSON 1

3. The Flood

By Genesis 6 mankind had become exceedingly wicked—so wicked that God wanted to destroy all of His creation. Can you understand how God would be willing to spare one family? To us, it would be easier to start over with someone who had never sinned and didn't know how wickedly man could behave. "But Noah found grace in the eyes of the Lord." God was willing to spare one family, a tremendous showing of grace. Notice that God saw Noah's righteousness even among all of the wickedness (Genesis 6:8). "... for thee have I seen righteous before me in this generation" (Genesis 7:1b). God sees us. He knows how we are living among a wicked generation. God gave man the free will to choose whether or not he would obey God. Understand the difference between one who belongs to God and one who does not. "But the natural man receiveth not the things of the Spirit of God: for they are foolishness unto him: neither can he know *them*, because they are spiritually discerned" (1 Corinthians 2:14).

Noah was probably joined by some of his godly family when he began building the ark. While he was building, he must have warned everyone of the coming flood. "And spared not the old world, but saved Noah the eighth *person*, a preacher of righteousness, bringing in the flood upon the world of the ungodly" (2 Peter 2:5). God spared Noah and his family.

LESSON 1   35   THE BIBLICAL PATH OF LIFE

"By faith Noah, being warned of God of things not seen as yet, moved with fear, prepared an ark to the saving of his house; by the which he condemned the world, and became heir of the righteousness which is by faith" (Hebrews 11:7).

"Which sometime were disobedient, when once the longsuffering of God waited in the days of Noah, while the ark was a preparing, wherein few, that is, eight souls were saved by water" (1 Peter 3:20).

We must be careful not to become "exceedingly wicked" in God's eyes. If we choose our will over God's, we are quickly becoming just that—exceedingly wicked. Remember what God did to His beautiful creation when mankind became exceedingly wicked (Genesis 6:5–7).

Noah prepared an ark to the saving of his house.

4. The Tower of Babel

By Genesis 11, the people had once again decided to choose what they wanted over what God told them to do. The people were of one language, and they found a plain and dwelt there. Then they decided to build themselves a city and a tower that would reach to heaven. They wanted to make a name for themselves, "…lest we be scattered abroad upon the face of the whole earth" (Genesis 11:4b). In Genesis 9:1, God told Noah and his sons to "be fruitful, and multiply, and replenish the earth." They couldn't do that if they stayed together and built a tower to make a name for themselves. Not for their Creator, the one who gave them life and all they would ever need to sustain that life, they choose to honor themselves. They did not even give God a chance to honor them. They disobeyed God's command. They wanted to do what they wanted and honor themselves. We should learn from this. We are not to build great things or places to honor ourselves.

We should seek honor from God only. "How can ye believe, which receive honour one of another, and seek not the honour that *cometh* from God only?" (John 5:44). We are to trust in God and believe in Him. Once again, God intervened in man's affairs. When they disobeyed God, He confused (confounded) their language so that they could not understand one another. It is interesting to note that the word *Babel* means "confusion."

They decided to build themselves a city and a tower that would reach to heaven.

LESSON 1   THE BIBLICAL PATH OF LIFE

A Deeper Path:

In Acts 2:4–8, 11–12, the languages were united so that the people could hear the Word of God. Where God confused their languages when the people wanted to make a name for themselves, God removed the language barrier so that they could hear Peter's sermon, where three thousand were saved (Acts 2:41).

Reinforcement:

After our lesson today, we cannot help but understand that we do not understand the things of God. We must learn to trust in the Lord with all our hearts and lean not to our understanding. (Remember today's key verse.)

Read the following scriptures, which you should easily understand after our study today. Faith is imperative to our trust in Jesus, and each of the people listed had faith. They all believed God's promise in Genesis 3:15, that he would send One, Jesus. They trusted God. Because of their faith, they were a "good report" for us to see as great examples. They should be our heroes in the faith.

1. Now faith is the substance of things hoped for, the evidence of things not seen. 2. For by it the elders obtained a good report. 3. Through faith we understand that the worlds were framed by the word of God, so that things which are seen were not made of things which do appear … 6. But without faith *it is* impossible to please *him*: for he that cometh to God must believe that he is, and *that* he is a rewarder of them that diligently seek him. 7. By faith Noah, being warned of God of things not seen as yet, moved with fear, prepared an ark to the saving of his house; by the which he condemned the world, and became heir of the righteousness which is by faith. (Hebrews 11:1–3, 6–7)

Think of a way that you have not yet trusted God, and write down at least one way you can begin to trust God in that area.

Closing:

It would be good to close with a short prayer reinforcing today's lesson. Always include any prayer requests you may have. *Today, pray for God to help us never to choose what we want to do instead of obeying God and His Word.*

LESSON 1

Genesis 1–11:4—Main Events
Creation, Fall, Flood, Babel

Read Genesis 1–11. Complete the following.

CREATION

1. Man was a special creation. How was he made? (Genesis 2:7)
_____
_____

2. Why did God make man? (Isaiah 43:7; Revelation 4:11) _____
_____
_____

3. Did God intend for man to work? (Genesis 2:15) _____
_____

4. What did God give man for food? (Genesis 1:29) _____
_____
_____

5. What was the one restriction placed on man? (Genesis 2:16–17)
_____
_____

THE FALL

6. Who tempted Eve? (Genesis 3:1) _____

_____

7. Who was the serpent? (Revelation 12:9) _____

_____

8. What happened when God came into the garden?(Genesis 3:8) _____

_____

9. Did God know where Adam and Eve were? _____ Wasn't God giving
them a chance to repent (to say they were sorry)? (Genesis 3:9)_____ Did they
do so? (Genesis 3:11–13) _____

10. Man was cursed for his sin (Genesis 3:14, 16–19). What was the promise of
deliverance? (Genesis 3:15**)** _____

THE FLOOD

11. By Genesis 6, what was the world like? (Genesis 6:5)_____

_____

12. How did God feel about the condition of the world? (Genesis 6:6–7) _____

_____

LESSON 1　**41**　THE BIBLICAL PATH OF LIFE

13. What happened when God looked upon Noah? (Genesis 6:8)
_____

14. What did God ask Noah to do? (Genesis 6:14) _____
Did Noah obey? _____

15. Who was saved by the ark? (Genesis 7:7) _____
_____

16. What was established from now on? (Genesis 8:22) _____
_____
_____

17. What did God command people to do? (Genesis 9:1, 7) _____
_____

THE TOWER OF BABEL

18. What did the people decide to do? (Genesis 11:3–4)_____
_____
_____

19. Did they obey God? (Genesis 9:1, 7) _____ Did they know they were disobeying? (Genesis 11:4)_____
_____

20. How had the people become before the flood? (Genesis 6:5) _____

_____

21. What could God see man becoming? (Genesis 11:6) _____

_____

_____

22. How did God prevent this from happening? (Genesis. 11:7–9) _____

_____

Answers:

1. God formed man of the dust of the ground, and breathed into his nostrils the breath of life; and man became a living soul; **2.** God created man for His glory, and for His pleasure; **3.** Yes; **4.** Every herb bearing seed and the fruit of every tree; **5.** They could eat freely of every tree of the garden—except for the tree of the knowledge of good and evil; **6.** The serpent; **7.** that old serpent, called the Devil and Satan; **8.** Adam and Eve hid from God; **9.** Yes; Yes; No; **10.** This is the first promise that God would send Jesus; **11.** The wickedness of man was great in the earth and every imagination of the thoughts of his heart was only evil continually. **12.** He was sorry he had made man, it grieved him at His heart, and he wanted to destroy man and all of the animals from the face of the earth; **13.** Noah found grace in the eyes of the Lord; **14.** Make an ark; Yes; **15.** Noah, his wife, and his son's wives; **16.** Seedtime and harvest, cold and heat, summer and winter, and day and night would not cease. God promised the seasons, nor day and night, would end; **17.** Be fruitful and multiply, and replenish the earth; and bring forth abundantly; **18.** Make brick, build a city and tower, and make a name for themselves; **19.** No; Yes, because they said "lest we be scattered abroad upon the face of the whole earth; **20.** Wicked and only evil continually; **21.** The people were one, and nothing would be restrained from what they imagined to do; **22.** God confounded (confused) their language so they couldn t understand each other—stopping the building process.)

LESSON 1 **43** THE BIBLICAL PATH OF LIFE

GENESIS 12–24
ABRAHAM AND ISAAC

LESSON 2

Key Verse

And the scripture was fulfilled which saith, Abraham believed God, and it was imputed unto him for righteousness: and he was called the Friend of God.

—JAMES 2:23

Key Verse Thought: Read today's key verse. Realize that *imputed* means "counted; to put to his account, either in his favor or what he must be answerable." *Righteousness* means "that righteousness which has regard to God and the divine law; especially internally where the heart is right with God; piety toward God, and hence righteousness; godliness; to count or impute as righteousness, i.e.: to regard as evidence of piety, hence the righteousness which is in or through faith in Christ." Noah is an example of where faith is counted as evidence of righteousness (Hebrews 11:7). Christ is presented as the source or author of righteousness (1 Corinthians 1:30). Thus, the righteousness of God means the righteousness that God approves, requires, or bestows. Those on whom God bestows His righteousness become righteous before God (2 Corinthians 5:21). Notice that James 2:23 is quoted from Genesis 15:6.

Emphasis: Righteousness before God is when we have faith in Jesus. "For he hath made him to *be* sin for us, who knew no sin; that we might be made the righteousness of God in him" (2 Corinthians 5:21).

Lesson Summary: Abraham believed the promise God made in Genesis 3:15 (God would send One to deliver mankind from their sins). It is proven in his faithfulness to obey God's call upon his life. He was faithful to leave his home and walk the land God promised would belong to his descendants (even though at this point he and Sarah were old and without any children). Abraham believed God would give him a son, just as He promised. Even when the promise was fulfilled and he had his son, Isaac, Abraham was faithful to obey God when God asked Abraham to give Isaac back. And because of Abraham's righteousness (faith that Jesus would come), he was called the Friend of God.

Suggested Bible Reading to Prepare for This Lesson

- Monday: **Genesis 12–13**
- Tuesday: **Genesis 14–15**
- Wednesday: **Genesis 16–17**
- Thursday: **Genesis 18–19**
- Friday: **Genesis 20–21**
- Saturday: **Genesis 22–24**

Genesis 12–24
Abraham and Isaac

① Abraham: Genesis 11:27–21:8

- Abraham called by God (Genesis 12:1–5)
- God's promises to Abraham (Genesis 15:5–6; 17:5–8; 22:15–18)
- The fulfillment of promise (Genesis 21:1–3)

② Abraham and Isaac: Genesis 21:1–28:5; 35:27–29

- The Son of promise (Genesis 21:1–3)
- God tests Abraham's faith/Isaac's obedience to his father (Genesis 22:1–18)
- A wife for Isaac (Genesis 24:2–4, 10–28, 61–67)
- Isaac's wife has twin boys (Genesis 25:19–27)

LESSON 2 47 THE BIBLICAL PATH OF LIFE

1. Abraham:
Genesis 11:27–21:8

We talked of the flood last week. Noah had three sons, from which all of the nations today have descended. Abram descended from Shem (Genesis 11:10, 26). Abram had a wife named Sarai. We later see that God changed their names (Genesis 17:5, 15). Abram is now known as Abraham, and his wife, Sarai, is now known as Sarah. Abram is Abraham, but we will continue to refer to him as Abraham.

God called Abraham to leave his home and his kindred to walk the land that God promised would belong to his descendants.

Abraham and Sarah leaving Ur with only a few belongings.

NOTICE: Abraham was seventy-five years old when God called him. His wife was also old (about sixty-five, past childbearing age), and they had no children, yet he trusted God's promise to give the land to his descendants. We notice another promise of Jesus at the time God calls Abraham (Genesis 12:2–3). "…and in thee shall all families of the earth be blessed" (Genesis 12:3). We see Jesus fulfill this: "25. Ye are the children of the prophets, and of the covenant which God made with our fathers, saying unto Abraham, And in thy seed shall all

THE BIBLICAL PATH OF LIFE   48   LESSON 2

the kindreds of the earth be blessed. 26. Unto you first God, having raised up his Son Jesus, sent him to bless you, in turning away every one of you from his iniquities" (Acts 3:25–26).

When Abraham obeyed God's words, God made a covenant with him. See it given to him twice.

- 14. And the LORD said unto Abram, after that Lot was separated from him, Lift up now thine eyes, and look from the place where thou art northward, and southward, and eastward, and westward: 15. For all the land which thou seest, to thee will I give it, and to thy seed for ever. 16. And I will make thy seed as the dust of the earth: so that if a man can number the dust of the earth, then shall thy seed also be numbered. 17. Arise, walk through the land in the length of it and in the breadth of it; for I will give it unto thee. 18. Then Abram removed his tent, and came and dwelt in the plain of Mamre, which is in Hebron, and built there an altar unto the LORD. (Genesis 13:14–18)

- 1. After these things the word of the LORD came unto Abram in a vision, saying, Fear not, Abram: I am thy shield, and thy exceeding great reward. 2. And Abram said, Lord GOD, what wilt thou give me, seeing I go childless, and the steward of my house is this Eliezer of Damascus? 3. And Abram said, Behold, to me thou hast given no seed: and, lo, one born in my house is mine heir. 4. And, behold, the word of the LORD came unto him, saying, This shall not be thine heir; but he that shall come forth out of thine own bowels shall be thine heir. 5. And he brought him forth abroad, and said, Look now

LESSON 2 **49** THE BIBLICAL PATH OF LIFE

toward heaven, and tell the stars, if thou be able to number them: and he said unto him, So shall thy seed be. (Genesis 15:1–5)

Abraham believed God's Word. "And he believed in the LORD; and he counted it to him for righteousness" (Genesis 15:6). And it was counted unto him for righteousness (refer back to the Key Verse Thought). Abraham continued to trust God and to walk with God. "And when Abram was ninety years old and nine, the LORD appeared to Abram, and said unto him, I am the Almighty God; walk before me, and be thou perfect" (Genesis 17:1). Help your students understand that Abraham was a sinful man, just like every other man, yet God considered him perfect. Perfect means "upright, sincere, or undefiled." Notice the things God promised Abraham in Genesis 17:6–8:

- I will make thee exceeding fruitful.
- I will make nations of thee.
- Kings shall come out of thee.
- To be a God unto thee, and to thy seed after thee.
- And I will give unto thee, and to thy seed after thee, the land wherein thou art a stranger, all the land of Canaan, for an everlasting possession; and I will be their God.

At least fifteen years had passed, and Abraham was now ninety years old (Genesis 17:1). Ten more years passed before God fulfilled his promise of a son.

1. And the LORD visited Sarah as he had said, and the LORD did unto Sarah as he had spoken. 2. For Sarah conceived, and bare Abraham a son in his old age, at the set time of which God had spoken to him. 3. And Abraham called the name of his son that

THE BIBLICAL PATH OF LIFE 50 LESSON 2

was born unto him, whom Sarah bare to him, Isaac. 4. And Abraham circumcised his son Isaac being eight days old, as God had commanded him. 5. And Abraham was an hundred years old, when his son Isaac was born unto him. 6. And Sarah said, God hath made me to laugh, so that all that hear will laugh with me. 7. And she said, Who would have said unto Abraham, that Sarah should have given children suck? for I have born him a son in his old age. 8. And the child grew, and was weaned: and Abraham made a great feast the same day that Isaac was weaned. (Genesis 21:1–8)

Birth of Isaac.

A Deeper Path:

In Genesis 16, we find what happened when man tried to hurry and fulfill God's plan of a son, for Sarah had Abraham marry her handmaiden, Hagar. Hagar conceived and gave birth to a son, Ishmael, which has always been an enemy of God's people, even until today.

In Genesis 18, we read of three men (from the Lord) who visited Abraham. This is when they told Abraham again that he would have a son, and when Sarah overheard from the tent, she laughed. These men also told Abraham of the imminent destruction of Sodom and Gomorrah for their wickedness, and the intercession on Abraham's behalf that saved Lot and his two daughters (found in Genesis 19).

LESSON 2 51 THE BIBLICAL PATH OF LIFE

2. Abraham and Isaac:
Genesis 21:1–28:5; 35:27–29

Read Genesis 22:1–18. God had a test for Abraham (the word *tempt* in Genesis 22:1 means "test, prove, or try"; refer to James 1:12–14). Notice that God provided a substitute offering for Abraham's son, Isaac, just as God provided a substitute offering for us because of our sins. Jesus was that offering. His death paid for our sins. Abraham never knew the picture his obedience would be to us, even today, of what God did with His own Son.

Read James 2:21–23. "21. Was not Abraham our father justified by works, when he had offered Isaac his son upon the altar? 22. Seest thou how faith wrought with his works, and by works was faith made perfect? 23. And the scripture was fulfilled which saith, Abraham believed God, and it was imputed unto him for righteousness: and he was called the Friend of God."

Abraham proved his great love for God by his act of obedience. He proved his worth to be called the Friend of God. Because of this act, see what God did to His promise.

"15. And the angel of the LORD called unto Abraham out of heaven the second time, 16. And said, By myself have I sworn, saith the LORD, for because thou hast done this thing, and hast not withheld thy son, thine only son: 17. That in blessing I will bless thee, and in multiplying I will multiply thy seed as the stars of the heaven, and as the sand which is upon the sea shore; and thy seed shall possess the gate of his enemies" (Genesis 22:15–17).

THE BIBLICAL PATH OF LIFE 52 LESSON 2

God doubled Abraham's blessing. Also notice yet another promise of Jesus' coming. "And in thy seed shall all the nations of the earth be blessed; because thou hast obeyed my voice" (Genesis 22:18).

And see it fulfilled in the following:

God doubled Abraham's blessing.

6. Even as Abraham believed God, and it was accounted to him for righteousness. 7. Know ye therefore that they which are of faith, the same are the children of Abraham. 8. And the scripture, foreseeing that God would justify the heathen through faith, preached before the gospel unto Abraham, *saying,* In thee shall all nations be blessed. 9. So then they which be of faith are blessed with faithful Abraham. …16. Now to Abraham and his seed were the promises made. He saith not, And to

seeds, as of many; but as of one, And to thy seed, which is Christ. …18. For if the inheritance *be* of the law, *it is* no more of promise: but God gave *it* to Abraham by promise. (Galatians 3:6–9, 16, 18)

Did you notice how Isaac acted through it all? He showed complete trust in his father. God's Word does not record any resistance (or complaints) on Isaac's part, not even when Abraham bound his son and prepared to sacrifice him. Isaac, too, proved himself during this time.

The New Testament gives us a little insight into this incident. "17. By faith Abraham, when he was tried, offered up Isaac: and he that had received the promises offered up his only begotten *son,* 18. Of whom it was said, That in Isaac shall thy seed be called: 19. Accounting that God was able to raise *him* up, even from the dead; from whence also he received him in a figure" (Hebrews 11:17–19).

Genesis 24 tells of Abraham's plan for Isaac to marry. Read the entire chapter. Take note of the finding of Rebekah, Isaac's wife. Notice how old Isaac

Isaac showed complete trust in his father.

THE BIBLICAL PATH OF LIFE 54 LESSON 2

was when he married. "And Isaac was forty years old when he took Rebekah to wife, the daughter of Bethuel the Syrian of Padanaram, the sister to Laban the Syrian" (Genesis 25:20).

Isaac and Rebekah had twin boys, Jacob and Esau.

21. And Isaac intreated the LORD for his wife, because she was barren: and the LORD was intreated of him, and Rebekah his wife conceived. 22. And the children struggled together within her; and she said, If it be so, why am I thus? And she went to enquire of the LORD. 23. And the LORD said unto her, Two nations are in thy womb, and two manner of people shall be separated from thy bowels; and the one people shall be stronger than the other people; and the elder shall serve the younger. 24. And when her days to be delivered were fulfilled, behold, there were twins in her womb. 25. And the first came out red, all over like an hairy garment; and they called his name Esau. 26. And after that came his brother out, and his hand took hold on Esau's heel; and his name was called Jacob: and Isaac was threescore years old when she bare them. 27. And the boys grew: and Esau was a cunning hunter, a man of the field; and Jacob was a plain man, dwelling in tents. (Genesis 25:20–27)

We will continue with Isaac and his sons next week.

Abraham was 175 years old when he died. "7. And these are the days of the years of Abraham's life which he lived, an hundred threescore and fifteen years. 8. Then Abraham gave up the ghost, and died in a good old age, an old man, and full *of years*; and was gathered to his people" (Genesis 25:7–8).

LESSON 2 **55** THE BIBLICAL PATH OF LIFE

Reinforcement:

Jesus asked a pertinent question: "When the Son of man cometh, shall he find faith on the earth?" As we have learned today, faith is believing Jesus came to take away our sins so we can be righteous in God's eyes. Noah and Abraham both had that kind of faith. Jesus' question should make us stop and think. Read the following verses:

8. …Nevertheless when the Son of man cometh, shall he find faith on the earth? 9. And he spake this parable unto certain which trusted in themselves that they were righteous, and despised others: 10. Two men went up into the temple to pray; the one a Pharisee, and the other a publican. 11. The Pharisee stood and prayed thus with himself, God, I thank thee, that I am not as other men *are*, extortioners, unjust, adulterers, or even as this publican. 12. I fast twice in the week, I give tithes of all that I possess. 13. And the publican, standing afar off, would not lift up so much as *his* eyes unto heaven, but smote upon his breast, saying, God be merciful to me a sinner. 14. I tell you, this man went down to his house justified *rather* than the other: for every one that exalteth himself shall be abased; and he that humbleth himself shall be exalted. 15. And they brought unto him also infants, that he would touch them: but when *his*

disciples saw *it,* they rebuked them. 16. But Jesus called them *unto him*, and said, Suffer little children to come unto me, and forbid them not: for of such is the kingdom of God. 17. Verily I say unto you, Whosoever shall not receive the kingdom of God as a little child shall in no wise enter therein. (Luke 18:8b–17)

Today, do we trust in ourselves for righteousness, as the Pharisees did, by comparing ourselves to other people? Or do we respond like the publican, who recognized he was sinner and asked for God's mercy. Jesus immediately called the children to Him. Unless we realize that it takes the faith "as a little child," we will never have the faith God requires by obedience with our entire lives.

Today, consider Abraham. Are you willing to change the course of your life to follow God, just as Abraham did?

Closing:

It would be good to close with a short prayer reinforcing today's lesson. Always include any prayer requests you may have. *Today, pray for God to help us have faith in Jesus, as Abraham, so we can be righteous before God.*

LESSON 2

Genesis 12–24:
Abraham and Isaac

Read Genesis 12–24.

1. What did God tell Abraham to do? Why? (Genesis 12:1–3) ____
_____
_____

2. Did Abraham obey? (Genesis 12:4–5) _____ How old was he? (Genesis 12:4) _____

3. What does the second promise of the Savior say? (Genesis 12:2–3)_____
_____Who does Acts 3:25–26 say is the one to bless and turn us from our iniquities?
_____

4. What did God promise Abraham? (Genesis 13:14–17; 15:4–5)
_____
_____
_____Did Abraham believe? (Genesis 15:6) _____

5. What did God tell him to do? (Genesis 17:1) _____
_____

THE BIBLICAL PATH OF LIFE   LESSON 2

6. Read Genesis 17:17. How old was Abraham? _____ How old was Sarah?

_____

7. What did Abraham and Sarah name this son of promise? (Genesis 21:3) _____ What did God tell Abraham to do with his son? (Genesis 22:1–2)

_____

_____ Did he obey? (Genesis

22:3)_____

8. Did Isaac offer any resistance to his dad's obedience to God, even when he didn't understand? (Genesis 22:7–9) _____ Who stopped Abraham from killing his son? (Genesis 22:11-12) _____ Why?

_____ What

was supplied for the offering instead? (Genesis 22:13) _____

9. What is said of Abraham because of his belief in God? (James 2:21–23)

_____

_____

10. What did God promise Abraham for his obedience? (Genesis 22:15–18)

_____

_____

_____

11. What did Abraham believe about God? (Hebrews 11:19) _____

_____

_____

LESSON 2 **59** THE BIBLICAL PATH OF LIFE

12. How did Isaac get a wife, and how old was he? (Genesis 24:2–4, 10–28; 25:20) _____

_____

_____

_____

13. What were Isaac's twin boys' names? (Genesis 25:19–27)
_____ and _____

Answers:

1. to leave his home and his kindred to walk the land; because God promised would belong to his descendants; **2.** Yes; 75 years old; **3.** and in thee shall all families of the earth be blessed; God's Son, Jesus; **4.** All of the land he could see would be given to him and his seed forever, and his descendants would be as the dust of the earth that cannot be numbered; his descendants would be as many as the stars in the sky; Yes; **5.** Walk before Him and be perfect; **6.** 100; 90; **7.** Isaac; to take his only son, Isaac, that he loved to a mountain in Moriah and offer him there for a burnt offering; Yes, Abraham took Isaac to offer him; **8.** No resistance is recorded in the Bible, only one question: where is the lamb for the offering?; the angel of the Lord called Abraham; because Abraham feared God and did not withhold his only son from the Lord; a ram; **9.** His faith was shown by his works, which made his faith perfect, and he was called the Friend of God; **10.** Not only would his descendants be as the stars of the heaven and the sands of the sea, but in his seed all of the nations of the earth would be blessed (the promise of Jesus); **11.** He believed God would raise Isaac from the dead; **12.** Abraham sent his servant back to his kindred to bring Isaac a wife, the servant went, prayed, and found Rebekah for him when Isaac was 40 years old; **13.** Esau and Jacob

THE BIBLICAL PATH OF LIFE 60 LESSON 2

GENESIS 25–36
JACOB

LESSON 3

Key Verse

He that overcometh shall inherit all things; and I will be his God, and he shall be my son.

—REVELATION 21:7

Key Verse Thought: This week we will study the change that took place in Jacob's life as he learned to trust God, inheriting the promise of Abraham. Make sure you understand the key verse and the importance of placing one's trust in God for victory. *Overcometh* means "conquer; subdue, coming from the root word nikē which is conquest, the means of success and victory." God always keeps His promises.

Emphasis: As we look at the life of Jacob, the third major person in the book of Genesis, focus on the importance of trusting God and understanding that He always keeps His promises.

Lesson Summary: Today we will remember the familiar Bible lessons of Jacob. He and Esau were twins. Jacob was the younger twin born to Isaac. God knew before Jacob was even born what kind of a man he would become, for he chose to walk with God. Because God had told Rebekah that Jacob would rule over Esau, she encouraged him to trick his father out of the family blessing, preempting God's plan. This caused contention, hatred, and grief from his brother for many years. Jacob had to flee for his life to another land. On the way, Jacob had a dream of angels ascending and descending a ladder into heaven. God spoke to him and gave him the promise of Abraham. Jacob obeyed his parents and chose a wife from his mother's family. But Jacob then was tricked by Laban, his mother's brother, who gave him the wrong daughter, Leah, in marriage. Jacob had to work fourteen years to gain the woman he loved, Rachel, Leah's sister.

The dream of Jacob.

When God told Jacob to return to his homeland, he obeyed. On the way, he

LESSON 3 **63** THE BIBLICAL PATH OF LIFE

wrestled with an angel of the Lord all night. It was the preincarnate Christ. During that struggle, Jacob was renamed Israel (which means *prince of God*). God blessed Jacob with twelve sons and at least one daughter. These sons became the twelve tribes of the nation Israel.

In the past two lessons, we saw where God promised to send One who would deliver a sinful people from their sins. The first was when man sinned in the garden (Genesis 3:15). Last week, we learned that God had promised Abraham that all people would be blessed through his descendants (Genesis 22:18). We even saw a picture (when Abraham offered Isaac) of what God would do—lay down the life of His Son, Jesus. In this lesson, we see once again the promise of a mighty Deliverer who would come (Genesis 28:14). Remember God's promise was fulfilled when He sent His Son, Jesus, to save the world from its sin. Jesus was the greatest gift ever given.

Suggested Bible Reading to Prepare for This Lesson

- ⊘ Monday: **Genesis 25–26**
- ⊘ Tuesday: **Genesis 27–28**
- ⊘ Wednesday: **Genesis 29–30**
- ⊘ Thursday: **Genesis 31–32**
- ⊘ Friday: **Genesis 33–34**
- ⊘ Saturday: **Genesis 35–36**

THE BIBLICAL PATH OF LIFE **64** LESSON 3

Genesis 25–36
Jacob

1 **Isaac and Rebekah's Sons (Genesis 25:19–34; 26:34–35)**

- Jacob and Esau born (Genesis 25:19–26)
- Natures revealed (Genesis 25:27–34; 26:34–35)

2 **Jacob and Esau (Genesis 27)**

- The trickery (Genesis 27:1–29)
- The tragedy (Genesis 27:30–45)

3 **Jacob Flees (Genesis 28–30)**

- God's promise (Genesis 28)
- Jacob's new home (Genesis 29–30)

4 **Jacob Became Israel (Genesis 31–32)**

- Jacob left for Canaan (Genesis 31)
- Jacob struggled with a man from the Lord (Genesis 32:24–32)

LESSON 3 **65** THE BIBLICAL PATH OF LIFE

1. Isaac and Rebekah's Sons
(Genesis 25:19–34; 26:34–35)

Last week we learned that Isaac and Rebekah had twin boys, Esau and Jacob.

19. And these are the generations of Isaac, Abraham's son: Abraham begat Isaac: 20. And Isaac was forty years old when he took Rebekah to wife, the daughter of Bethuel the Syrian of Padanaram, the sister to Laban the Syrian. 21. And Isaac intreated the LORD for his wife, because she was barren: and the LORD was intreated of him, and Rebekah his wife conceived. 22. And the children struggled together within her; and she said, If *it be* so, why *am* I thus? And she went to enquire of the LORD. 23. And the LORD said unto her, Two nations *are* in thy womb, and two manner of people shall be separated from thy bowels; and *the one* people shall be stronger than *the other* people; and the elder shall serve the younger. 24. And when her days to be delivered were fulfilled, behold, *there were* twins in her womb. 25. And the first came out red, all over like an hairy garment; and they called his name Esau. 26. And after that came his brother out, and his hand took hold on Esau's heel; and his name was called Jacob: and Isaac *was* threescore years old when she bare them. (Genesis 25:19–26)

THE BIBLICAL PATH OF LIFE 66 LESSON 3

Esau was the older, and Jacob was born holding onto Esau's heel. The strife and contention between these two brothers began before their birth (Genesis 25:22–23). God knew before they were born that two nations would be born from Rebekah's womb. And remember what we just read—that God had told Rebekah, "Two nations are in thy womb, and two manner of people shall be separated from thy bowels; and *the one* people shall be stronger than *the other* people; and the elder shall serve the younger." Rebekah listened to God.

See the natures of Esau and Jacob revealed.

27. And the boys grew: and Esau was a cunning hunter, a man of the field; and Jacob *was* a plain man, dwelling in tents. 28. And Isaac loved Esau, because he did eat of *his* venison: but Rebekah loved Jacob. 29. And Jacob sod pottage: and Esau came from the field, and he was faint: 30. And Esau said to Jacob, Feed me, I pray thee, with that same red *pottage*; for I *am* faint: therefore was his name called Edom. 31. And Jacob said, Sell me this day thy birthright. 32. And Esau said, Behold, I am at the point to die: and what profit shall this birthright do to me? 33. And Jacob said, Swear

Rebekah loved her son Jacob, the man who would walk with God.

LESSON 3 67 THE BIBLICAL PATH OF LIFE

to me this day; and he sware unto him: and he sold his birthright unto Jacob. 34. Then Jacob gave Esau bread and pottage of lentiles; and he did eat and drink, and rose up, and went his way: thus Esau despised *his* birthright. (Genesis 25:27–34)

Esau was red and hairy and was growing to become a skillful hunter, a man of the field. Jacob was the second born. *Plain* means "complete; whole; upright—always in a moral sense; having integrity, mild; harmless; quiet." He was "a plain man"—quiet, mild, or upright. God knew the kind of man Esau would become even before he was born. He also knew what kind of man Jacob would become. God chose the man who would walk with Him and serve Him (Jacob) over the man who would serve his own flesh rather than follow God. It was evidenced early in these brothers' lives, when Esau was willing to readily sell his birthright (Genesis 25:30–34). Esau would rather have instant gratification (to appease his hunger) than the lasting benefits of the birthright. The contention between these brothers continued, not only throughout their lives but among their descendants. Much of the suffering of the Israelites (Jacob's descendants) came at the hands of the Edomites (Esau's descendants), as we will see throughout the Old Testament (Numbers 20:20, 21; 2 Samuel 8:13–14; Psalm 137:7), and even into the New Testament (Herod was an Edomite who killed the babes of Bethlehem, wanting to kill Jesus. See Matthew 2:16). Read God's Word on the matter. "As it is written, Jacob have I loved, but Esau have I hated" (Romans 9:13).

Esau chose to do what he wanted, displeasing God and his parents. "34. And Esau was forty years old when he took to wife Judith the daughter of Beeri the Hittite, and Bashemath the daughter of Elon the Hittite: 35. Which were a grief of mind unto Isaac and to Rebekah" (Genesis 26:34–35).

2. Jacob and Esau
(Genesis 27)

Read Genesis 27 to remember the events when Rebekah and Jacob tricked Isaac and Esau out of the blessing. Isaac sent Esau to the field to kill some venison to prepare for him. He wanted to bless Esau before he died (see Genesis 27:1–4). But Rebekah heard about it and devised plans of her own.

> 5. And Rebekah heard when Isaac spake to Esau his son. And Esau went to the field to hunt *for* venison, and to bring *it*. 6. And Rebekah spake unto Jacob her son, saying, Behold, I heard thy father speak unto Esau thy brother, saying, 7. Bring me venison, and make me savoury meat, that I may eat, and bless thee before the LORD before my death. 8. Now therefore, my son, obey my voice according to that which I command thee. 9. Go now to the flock, and fetch me from thence two good kids of the goats; and I will make them savoury meat for thy father, such as he loveth: 10. And thou shalt bring *it* to thy father, that he may eat, and that he may bless thee before his death. (Genesis 27:5–10)

If you remember, God had told Rebekah that Esau would serve Jacob (Genesis 25:23), but she didn't wait upon God. Remember Jacob's initial response: "11. And Jacob said to Rebekah his mother, Behold, Esau my brother *is* a hairy

LESSON 3 **69** THE BIBLICAL PATH OF LIFE

man, and I *am* a smooth man: 12. My father peradventure will feel me, and I shall seem to him as a deceiver; and I shall bring a curse upon me, and not a blessing. 13. And his mother said unto him, Upon me *be* thy curse, my son: only obey my voice, and go fetch me *them*" (Genesis 27:11–13).

And then we see his obedience. "14. And he went, and fetched, and brought *them* to his mother: and his mother made savoury meat, such as his father loved. 15. And Rebekah took goodly raiment of her eldest son Esau, which *were* with her in the house, and put them upon Jacob her younger son: 16. And she put the skins of the kids of the goats upon his hands, and upon the smooth of his neck: 17. And she gave the savoury meat and the bread, which she had prepared, into the hand of her son Jacob" (Genesis 27:14–17).

Then Jacob went in to see his father.

18. And he came unto his father, and said, My father: and he said, Here *am* I; who *art* thou, my son? 19. And Jacob said unto his father, I *am* Esau thy firstborn; I have done according as thou badest me: arise, I pray thee, sit and eat of my venison, that thy soul may bless me. 20. And Isaac said unto his son, How *is it* that thou hast found *it* so quickly, my son? And he said, Because the LORD thy God brought *it* to me. 21. And Isaac said unto Jacob, Come near, I pray thee, that I may feel thee, my son, whether thou *be* my very son Esau or not. 22. And Jacob went near unto Isaac his father; and he felt him, and said, The voice *is* Jacob's voice, but the hands *are* the hands of Esau. 23. And he discerned him not, because his hands were hairy, as his brother Esau's hands: so he blessed him. 24. And he said, *Art* thou my very son Esau? And he

said, I *am*. 25. And he said, Bring *it* near to me, and I will eat of my son's venison, that my soul may bless thee. And he brought *it* near to him, and he did eat: and he brought him wine, and he drank. 26. And his father Isaac said unto him, Come near now, and kiss me, my son. (Genesis 27:18–26)

Isaac blessed Jacob, believing he was Esau (Genesis 27:27–29). But then Esau returned.

30. And it came to pass, as soon as Isaac had made an end of blessing Jacob, and Jacob was yet scarce gone out from the presence of Isaac his father, that Esau his brother came in from his hunting. 31. And he also had made savoury meat, and brought it unto his father, and said unto his father, Let my father arise, and eat of his son's venison, that thy soul may bless me. 32. And Isaac his father said unto him, Who *art* thou? And he said, I *am* thy son, thy firstborn Esau. 33. And Isaac trembled very exceedingly, and said, Who? where *is* he that hath taken venison, and brought *it* me, and I have eaten of all before thou camest, and have blessed him? yea, *and* he shall

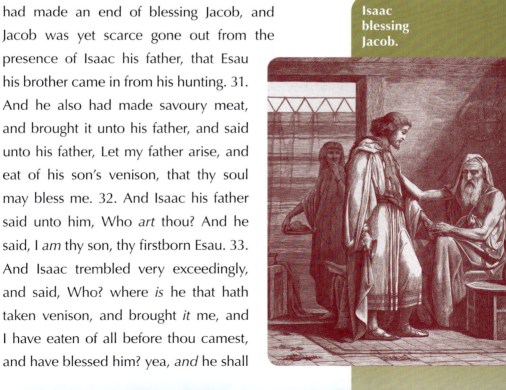

Isaac blessing Jacob.

LESSON 3   71   THE BIBLICAL PATH OF LIFE

be blessed. 34. And when Esau heard the words of his father, he cried with a great and exceeding bitter cry, and said unto his father, Bless me, *even* me also, O my father. 35. And he said, Thy brother came with subtilty, and hath taken away thy blessing. (Genesis 27:30–35)

Esau was angry with Jacob for taking his birthright and then his blessing. "And he said, Is not he rightly named Jacob? for he hath supplanted me these two times: he took away my birthright; and, behold, now he hath taken away my blessing. And he said, Hast thou not reserved a blessing for me?" (Genesis 27:36).

See the words Isaac had for his son, Esau, in the following:

37. And Isaac answered and said unto Esau, Behold, I have made him thy lord, and all his brethren have I given to him for servants; and with corn and wine have I sustained him: and what shall I do now unto thee, my son? 38. And Esau said unto his father, Hast thou but one blessing, my father? bless me, *even* me also, O my father. And Esau lifted up his voice, and wept. 39. And Isaac his father answered and said unto him, Behold, thy dwelling shall be the fatness of the earth, and of the dew of heaven from above; 40. And by thy sword shalt thou live, and shalt serve thy brother; and it shall come to pass when thou shalt have the dominion, that thou shalt break his yoke from off thy neck. (Genesis 27:37–40)

Notice that Esau would serve his younger brother. "And Esau hated

THE BIBLICAL PATH OF LIFE 72 LESSON 3

Jacob because of the blessing wherewith his father blessed him: and Esau said in his heart, The days of mourning for my father are at hand; then will I slay my brother Jacob" (Genesis 27:41). Esau wanted to kill Jacob and promised to do so as soon as his father died.

Because of this trickery and his brother's hatred of him, Jacob had to leave home, fleeing for his life.

> 42. And these words of Esau her elder son were told to Rebekah: and she sent and called Jacob her younger son, and said unto him, Behold, thy brother Esau, as touching thee, doth comfort himself, purposing to kill thee. 43. Now therefore, my son, obey my voice; and arise, flee thou to Laban my brother to Haran; 44. And tarry with him a few days, until thy brother's fury turn away; 45. Until thy brother's anger turn away from thee, and he forget that which thou hast done to him: then I will send, and fetch thee from thence: why should I be deprived also of you both in one day? (Genesis 27:42–45)

Be encouraged that although God's plan was for Jacob to rule over Esau (Genesis 24:23), this trickery was Rebekah's plan. She had *listened* to God but because she did not *wait* upon God to work, much conflict and heartache came. Rebekah died before Jacob could return home, so Jacob never saw his mother again.

3. Jacob Flees
(Genesis 28–30)

Before Isaac sent Jacob away from home, he instructed him and blessed him again.

> 1. And Isaac called Jacob, and blessed him, and charged him, and said unto him, Thou shalt not take a wife of the daughters of Canaan. 2. Arise, go to Padanaram, to the house of Bethuel thy mother's father; and take thee a wife from thence of the daughters of Laban thy mother's brother. 3. And God Almighty bless thee, and make thee fruitful, and multiply thee, that thou mayest be a multitude of people; 4. And give thee the blessing of Abraham, to thee, and to thy seed with thee; that thou mayest inherit the land wherein thou art a stranger, which God gave unto Abraham. 5. And Isaac sent away Jacob: and he went to Padanaram unto Laban, son of Bethuel the Syrian, the brother of Rebekah, Jacob's and Esau's mother. (Genesis 28:1–5)

Once again we see the true nature of Jacob and Esau revealed. "7. And that Jacob obeyed his father and his mother, and was gone to Padanaram; 8. And Esau seeing that the daughters of Canaan pleased not Isaac his father; 9. Then went Esau unto Ishmael, and took unto the wives which he had Mahalath the daughter of Ishmael Abraham's son, the sister of Nebajoth, to be his wife"

THE BIBLICAL PATH OF LIFE **74** LESSON 3

(Genesis 28:7–9). Jacob obeyed his parents, and Esau chose purposefully to displease his parents. "And Jacob went out from Beersheba, and went toward Haran" (Genesis 28:10).

On his way, when Jacob stopped to rest at night, he had a dream.

11. And he lighted upon a certain place, and tarried there all night, because the sun was set; and he took of the stones of that place, and put *them for* his pillows, and lay down in that place to sleep. 12. And he dreamed, and behold a ladder set up on the earth, and the top of it reached to heaven: and behold the angels of God ascending and descending on it. 13. And, behold, the LORD stood above it, and said, I *am* the LORD God of Abraham thy father, and the God of Isaac: the land whereon thou liest, to thee will I give it, and to thy seed; 14. And thy seed shall be as the dust of the earth, and thou shalt spread abroad to the west, and to the east, and to the north, and to the south: and in thee and in thy seed shall all the families of the earth be blessed.

Jacob's ladder.

LESSON 3   75   THE BIBLICAL PATH OF LIFE

15. And, behold, I *am* with thee, and will keep thee in all *places* whither thou goest, and will bring thee again into this land; for I will not leave thee, until I have done *that* which I have spoken to thee of. (Genesis 28:11–15)

In this dream, God came to him and gave him the promise of Abraham.

NOTE

Genesis 28:14 ("…and in thee and in thy seed shall all the families of the earth be blessed") is a *promise of Jesus.* "25. Ye are the children of the prophets, and of the covenant which God made with our fathers, saying unto Abraham, And in thy seed shall all the kindreds of the earth be blessed. 26. Unto you first God, having raised up his Son Jesus, sent him to bless you, in turning away every one of you from his iniquities" (Acts 3:25–26). Jacob then committed himself to God (Genesis 28:16–22). Especially note the promise Jacob made.

18. And Jacob rose up early in the morning, and took the stone that he had put *for* his pillows, and set it up

for a pillar, and poured oil upon the top of it. 19. And he called the name of that place Bethel: but the name of that city *was called* Luz at the first. 20. And Jacob vowed a vow, saying, If God will be with me, and will keep me in this way that I go, and will give me bread to eat, and raiment to put on, 21. So that I come again to my father's house in peace; then shall the LORD be my God: 22. And this stone, which I have set *for* a pillar, shall be God's house: and of all that thou shalt give me I will surely give the tenth unto thee. (Genesis 28:18–22)

Notice that Jacob named the place Bethel, and he promised to return.

When Jacob reached the land of his kindred, he did as his parents told him to do; he planned to take a wife of his people. But his future father-in-law, Laban, tricked him. He was Rebekah's brother (Genesis 25:20). Jacob agreed to work for Laban for seven years to marry his daughter, Rachel. But instead, Laban intentionally gave Jacob the wrong daughter, Leah, for a wife. He then had to work an additional seven years to marry Rachel.   Jacob ended up with both sisters as his wives (Genesis 29:1–30)

God told Jacob to go back home. "And the LORD said unto Jacob, Return unto the land of thy fathers, and to thy kindred; and I will be with thee" (Genesis 31:3). And Jacob obeyed. "17. Then Jacob rose up, and set his sons and his wives upon camels; 18. And he carried away all his cattle, and all his goods which he had gotten, the cattle of his getting, which he had gotten in Padanaram, for to go to Isaac his father in the land of Canaan" (Genesis 31:17–18).

Jacob began the return to the land of his father, Isaac.

LESSON 3   **77**   THE BIBLICAL PATH OF LIFE

4. Jacob Became Israel
(Genesis 31–36)

Here's what happened on the way back:

24. And Jacob was left alone; and there wrestled a man with him until the breaking of the day. 25. And when he saw that he prevailed not against him, he touched the hollow of his thigh; and the hollow of Jacob's thigh was out of joint, as he wrestled with him. 26. And he said, Let me go, for the day breaketh. And he said, I will not let thee go, except thou bless me. 27. And he said unto him, What is thy name? And he said, Jacob. 28. And he said, Thy name shall be called no more Jacob, but Israel: for as a prince hast thou power with God and with men, and hast prevailed. 29. And Jacob asked *him*, and said, Tell *me,* I pray thee, thy name. And he said, Wherefore *is* it that thou dost ask after my name? And he blessed him there. 30. And Jacob called the name of the place Peniel: for I have seen God face to face, and my life is preserved. 31. And as he passed over Penuel the sun rose upon him, and he halted upon his thigh. 32. Therefore the children of Israel eat not *of* the sinew which shrank, which *is* upon the hollow of the thigh, unto this day: because he touched the hollow of Jacob's thigh in the sinew that shrank. (Genesis 32:24–32)

That man was the preincarnate Christ. It was here that God renamed Jacob. He became Israel. *Israel* means "he will rule as God." God had blessed Jacob (now Israel) with twelve sons and one daughter. Israel's sons became the twelve tribes of the nation Israel. This was another part of the promise God had made to Adam and Even in the garden, Abraham, Rebekah, and Jacob.

Jacob returning to Bethel.

The following is a list of Jacob's sons in birth order (see also Genesis 35:23–26):

1. Reuben
2. Simeon
3. Levi (the priestly tribe)
4. Judah (the kingly tribe)
5. Dan
6. Naphtali
7. Gad
8. Asher
9. Issachar
10. Zebulun
11. Joseph
12. Benjamin

God came to Jacob again and blessed him. God reaffirmed His promise to Jacob, now Israel, and his sons.

LESSON 1   THE BIBLICAL PATH OF LIFE

9. And God appeared unto Jacob again, when he came out of Padanaram, and blessed him. 10. And God said unto him, Thy name *is* Jacob: thy name shall not be called any more Jacob, but Israel shall be thy name: and he called his name Israel. 11. And God said unto him, I *am* God Almighty: be fruitful and multiply; a nation and a company of nations shall be of thee, and kings shall come out of thy loins; 12. And the land which I gave Abraham and Isaac, to thee I will give it, and to thy seed after thee will I give the land. 13. And God went up from him in the place where he talked with him. 14. And Jacob set up a pillar in the place where he talked with him, *even* a pillar of stone: and he poured a drink offering thereon, and he poured oil thereon. 15. And Jacob called the name of the place where God spake with him, Bethel. (Genesis 35:9–15)

Jacob had fulfilled the promise to return to Bethel that he made after the dream God gave him of the angels ascending and descending from heaven (see Genesis 28:11–22).

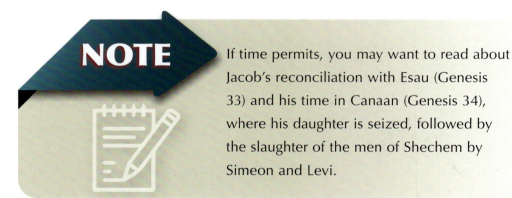

If time permits, you may want to read about Jacob's reconciliation with Esau (Genesis 33) and his time in Canaan (Genesis 34), where his daughter is seized, followed by the slaughter of the men of Shechem by Simeon and Levi.

Reinforcement:

In the past two lessons, we have seen where God promised to send One who would deliver a sinful people from their sins. The first was when man sinned in the garden (Genesis 3:15). Last week, we learned that God promised Abraham that all people would be blessed through his descendants (Genesis 22:18). We even saw a picture (in Abraham and Isaac) of what God would do—lay down the life of His Son. This week, we saw once again the promise of a mighty Deliverer who would come (Genesis 28:14). God even changed Jacob's name to Israel, indicating that it would be through the seed of one of his sons that God's Promised One would come. Help your students understand that God planned to send His Son, Jesus, from the beginning, and he constantly reminded mankind that He would come.

Again, remember that Jesus is God's greatest gift.

Closing:

It would be good to close with a short prayer reinforcing today's lesson. Always include any prayer requests you may have. *Today, pray for God to help us recognize that the gift of Jesus was promised from the beginning as the only way to be delivered from our sins. He was the greatest gift ever given.*

LESSON 3   THE BIBLICAL PATH OF LIFE

LESSON 3

Genesis 25–32: Jacob

Complete the following.

1. What did God tell Rebekah about her twin boys before they were born? (Genesis 25:23 _____

_____

_____

2. How does the Bible describe Esau? (Genesis 25:25, 27) _____

_____

How does the Bible describe Jacob? (Genesis 25:27) _____

_____

3. What did Esau give up for bread and pottage? (Genesis 25:29–34)

Esau chose to temporarily satisfy his hunger rather than have the lasting benefit of his birthright.

4. Remembering what God told Rebekah about the younger ruling the older, what did Rebekah have Jacob do? (Genesis 27:1–29)

_____

_____ Was that right? _____

What problems came from this trickery? _____

_____

THE BIBLICAL PATH OF LIFE 82 LESSON 3

5. What did Isaac send Jacob to do? (Genesis 28:1–2) _____

_____

_____ Did he obey? (Genesis 28:7) _____

6. Whose blessing was Jacob to receive? (Genesis 28:3–4) _____

_____

What was that blessing? _____

_____

7. On his journey, what did Jacob dream? (Genesis 28:10–15) _____

_____ What part of this blessing sounds familiar?

_____

To whom was this blessing given to first? (Genesis 12:1–3) _____

Remember: This "blessing" is the promise of Jesus
(see Acts 3:25–26).

8. What was Jacob willing to do to marry Rachel? (Genesis 29:18)_____

_____ What did Laban, Rachel's dad, do?

(Genesis 29:21–25) _____

_____

How long did Jacob end up working to marry Rachel? (Genesis 29:30) _____

9. What did God tell Jacob to do? (Genesis 31:3) _____

_____

_____

_____

LESSON 3 **83** THE BIBLICAL PATH OF LIFE

10. On the way home, Jacob was left alone at night. What happened? (Genesis 32:24–28) _____

_____

When Jacob saw "God face to face" (Genesis 32:30), this was the preincarnate Christ (that is, Jesus before He was born as a man on earth).

Answers:

1. Two nations and two manner of people would be born, one people would be stronger than the other, and the elder would serve the younger;

2. Esau was red, hairy, and a skillful hunter; a man of the field; Jacob was plain, quiet, mild, or upright, dwelling in tents;

3. his birthright;

4. Jacob pretended to be Esau to trick his dad into giving him the blessing, or inheritance; no; division among the family; Esau hated Jacob and wanted to kill him, and Jacob had to flee for his life;

5. to go take a wife from Rebekah's family; yes;

6. The blessing God gave to Abraham; that God would bless him and multiply him so that he would be a multitude of people;

7. A ladder to heaven with angels ascending and descending; God promised the land, that his seed would be as the dust of the earth, and that in his seed all of the families of the earth would be blessed;

8. Work seven years for Laban; gave him Leah instead of Rachel; fourteen years;

9. Return to the land of his fathers;

10. Jacob wrestled with a man all night, refusing to let go until he was blessed. Jacob's name was changed to Israel, and Jacob realized he had seen God face to face.

THE BIBLICAL PATH OF LIFE **84** LESSON 3

GENESIS 37–50
JOSEPH

LESSON 4

Key Verse

For the wages of sin is death; but the gift of God is eternal life through Jesus Christ our Lord.

—ROMANS 6:23

Key Verse Thought: Understand the key verse and the importance of recognizing the greatest gift God ever gave—His Son, Jesus—to pay the penalty for our sins.

Emphasis: Recognize God's blessings upon Joseph's life, for although he endured many problems (his brothers hated him; he was sold into slavery; he was falsely imprisoned and forgotten; and so on), he remained faithful to God. And God blessed Joseph's life. Joseph was the last major person in the book of Genesis.

Lesson Summary: Today we will remember the familiar Bible lessons of Jacob and one of his sons, Joseph. Joseph was the eleventh son and the last to be born to Jacob before he returned to the land promised to Abraham and Isaac. Joseph was a godly young man in spite of adverse circumstances in his life. God used him to save his family from starvation during a time of famine throughout the lands.

In the Old Testament, Joseph is one of the people we compare to a picture of Christ. In the past few lessons, we have seen where God promised to send One who would deliver a sinful people from their sins. The first time was when man sinned in the garden (Genesis 3:15), and then we saw God promise Abraham that all people would be blessed through his descendants (Genesis 22:18). We even saw a picture of what God would do—lay down the life of His Son. In this lesson, we see once again the promise of a mighty Deliverer who would come (Genesis 28:14). And better yet, we see a *picture* of a mighty deliverer in Jacob's son, Joseph. When Joseph's brothers sold him into slavery, they meant it for evil. "But as for you, ye thought evil against me; *but* God meant it unto good, to bring to pass, as *it is* this day, to save much people alive" (Genesis 50:20). God sent His Son, Jesus, to save the world from their sin. He was the greatest gift ever given. But sinful man crucified him (evil against Him), and God took what man *intended* to be evil and delivered us from our sins by Jesus' death. Just as Joseph recognized that he was placed in a position to save the world from starvation, Jesus came to save the world from "the wages of sin … death" and instead give us the "gift of God … eternal life through Jesus Christ our Lord." Notice the faithfulness of Joseph and the blessings of God upon him.

Suggested Bible Reading to Prepare for This Lesson

⊘ Monday:	**Genesis 37–39**	⊘ Thursday:	**Genesis 45–46**
⊘ Tuesday:	**Genesis 40–42**	⊘ Friday:	**Genesis 47–48**
⊘ Wednesday:	**Genesis 43–44**	⊘ Saturday:	**Genesis 49–50**

LESSON 4   87   THE BIBLICAL PATH OF LIFE

Genesis 37–50:
Joseph

1 ## Joseph, the Dreamer (Genesis 37)

- Joseph, the favorite son of his father
- Joseph, hated by his brothers

2 ## Joseph, the Slave (Genesis 39:1–20)

- Blessed by God
- Betrayed by Potiphar's wife

3 ## Joseph, the Prisoner (Genesis 39:21–40:40)

- Blessed by God
- Forgotten by the butler
- Pharaoh's dream

4 ## Joseph, the Ruler (Genesis 40:41–50:26)

- Blessed by God
- Savior to the world

5. Joseph, an Old Testament Picture of Christ

- Compare Joseph with Jesus

1. Joseph, the Dreamer
(Genesis 37)

Joseph was the eleventh son born to Jacob (Genesis 37:2). He was born of Rachel, the woman whom Jacob loved so much that he worked fourteen years for his father-in-law so he could marry her. Joseph was seventeen years old at the time of the following occurrence: "3. Now Israel loved Joseph more than all his children, because he *was* the son of his old age: and he made him a coat of *many* colours. 4. And when his brethren saw that their father loved him more than all his brethren, they hated him, and could not speak peaceably unto him." (Genesis 37:3–4). Joseph was the firstborn son of the woman Jacob loved, which probably explains why Jacob loved him more than any of the sons born before him. This special love made his brothers hate him. Jacob gave Joseph a special coat of many colors to show this love. It didn't help that when Joseph's brothers did evil, he reported those instances to their father (Genesis 37:2).

Joseph dreamed and told these dreams to his family.

> 5. And Joseph dreamed a dream, and he told *it* his brethren: and they hated him yet the more. 6. And he said unto them, Hear, I pray you, this dream which I have dreamed: 7. For, behold, we *were* binding sheaves in the field, and, lo, my sheaf arose, and also stood upright; and, behold, your sheaves stood round about, and made obeisance to my sheaf. 8. And his brethren said to him, Shalt thou indeed reign over us? or shalt

thou indeed have dominion over us? And they hated him yet the more for his dreams, and for his words. 9. And he dreamed yet another dream, and told it his brethren, and said, Behold, I have dreamed a dream more; and, behold, the sun and the moon and the eleven stars made obeisance to me. 10. And he told *it* to his father, and to his brethren: and his father rebuked him, and said unto him, What *is* this dream that thou hast dreamed? Shall I and thy mother and thy brethren indeed come to bow down ourselves to thee to the earth? 11. And his brethren envied him; but his father observed the saying. (Genesis 37:5–11)hen she bare them. (Genesis 25:19–26)

Joseph telling his dream to his father.

For this, his brothers hated him more. This was an intense hatred that created the desire to have no relationship or contact with the one hated. Their *envy* (Genesis 37:11) means they desired what Joseph had.

LESSON 4   91   THE BIBLICAL PATH OF LIFE

Read Genesis 37:12–36 to refresh your memory on the brothers selling Joseph into slavery. Remember that Joseph was obeying his father (checking on his brothers). When the brothers saw him coming, "…they conspired against him to slay him" (Genesis 37:18b). Read their plan to kill him and Reuben's plea for Joseph's life in Genesis 37:20–22. But when the brothers saw "…a company of Ishmeelites came from Gilead with their camels bearing spicery and balm and myrrh, going to carry it down to Egypt" (Genesis 37:25b), they decided to sell him for a profit instead. Notice that Reuben was not part of this plan. "And Reuben returned unto the pit; and, behold, Joseph was not in the pit; and he rent his clothes" (Genesis 37:29).

The brothers plotted together to bring Joseph's coat of many colors, given to him by his father, covered with blood and give it to their father, Jacob (Israel). And that is what they did. Read Jacob's response to the sight of the blood-covered coat. "33. And he knew it, and said, *It* is my son's coat; an evil beast hath devoured him; Joseph is without doubt rent in pieces. 34. And Jacob rent his clothes, and put sackcloth upon his loins, and mourned for his son many days" (Genesis 37:33–34). Jacob believed his son Joseph was dead.

Joseph sold by his brothers.

THE BIBLICAL PATH OF LIFE · 92 · LESSON 4

2. Joseph, the Slave
(Genesis 39:1–20)

But Joseph was not dead. "And Joseph was brought down to Egypt; and Potiphar, an officer of Pharaoh, captain of the guard, an Egyptian, bought him of the hands of the Ishmeelites, which had brought him down thither" (Genesis 39:1). Joseph was now a slave in the Egyptian Potiphar's house. "And the LORD was with Joseph, and he was a prosperous man; and he was in the house of his master the Egyptian" (Genesis 39:2). See that Potiphar recognized that God was with Joseph. "And his master saw that the LORD was with him, and that the LORD made all that he did to prosper in his hand" (Genesis 39:3). Because of this, Potiphar made Joseph overseer of his house, and the Lord blessed Potiphar's house because of Joseph. See how the Bible describes Joseph: "…And Joseph was a goodly *person*, and well favoured" (Genesis 39:6b).

Read Genesis 39:7–20 to remember why Joseph was thrown into prison.

Recognize that no matter what circumstance Joseph was in, he chose to do what was right, and God blessed him for it.

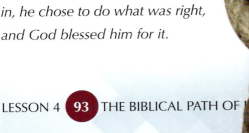

LESSON 4   93   THE BIBLICAL PATH OF

3. Joseph, the Prisoner
(Genesis 39:21–40:40)

Joseph faithful in prison.

Joseph was unjustly thrown into prison. "21. But the LORD was with Joseph, and shewed him mercy, and gave him favour in the sight of the keeper of the prison. 22. And the keeper of the prison committed to Joseph's hand all the prisoners that were in the prison; and whatsoever they did there, he was the doer *of it*. 23. The keeper of the prison looked not to any thing *that was* under his hand; because the LORD was with him, and *that* which he did, the LORD made *it* to prosper" (Genesis 39:21–23). Joseph was a godly witness before the prison guard and the other prisoners. They recognized the difference of a young man with God in his life, especially the prison guard, for he placed Joseph over all of the prisoners.

The pharaoh's butler and baker were both

THE BIBLICAL PATH OF LIFE 94 LESSON 4

prisoners. Joseph tended to them. When he recognized that they were troubled, he asked what was wrong. Both of them had had troubling dreams (read the dreams and Joseph's interpretations from God in Genesis 40:8–20). Not only did Joseph tell them what their dreams meant, but they both witnessed the fulfillment of these dreams. "20. And it came to pass the third day, *which was Pharaoh's birthday*, that he made a feast unto all his servants: and he lifted up the head of the chief butler and of the chief baker among his servants. 21. And he restored the chief butler unto his butlership again; and he gave the cup into Pharaoh's hand: 22. But he hanged the chief baker: as Joseph had interpreted to them" (Genesis 40:20–22).

Joseph had made a simple request. "14. But think on me when it shall be well with thee, and shew kindness, I pray thee, unto me, and make mention of me unto Pharaoh, and bring me out of this house: 15. For indeed I was stolen away out of the land of the Hebrews: and here also have I done nothing that they should put me into the dungeon … 23. Yet did not the chief butler remember Joseph, but forgat him" (Genesis 40:14–15, 23).

Even when Joseph was in prison, God was working in his life, bringing Joseph to the place God wanted him to be.

The Lord was with Joseph when he was in prison.

LESSON 4   95   THE BIBLICAL PATH OF LIFE

4. Joseph, the Ruler
(Genesis 40:41–50:26)

Because Joseph was in the prison when the butler and baker had their dreams, he was able to tell them not only what the dreams meant but see the fulfillment of those dreams, exactly as Joseph had told them. When the day came that Pharaoh had a troubling dream that no one could interpret for him, the butler remembered Joseph.

> 9. Then spake the chief butler unto Pharaoh, saying, I do remember my faults this day: 10. Pharaoh was wroth with his servants, and put me in ward in the captain of the guard's house, *both* me and the chief baker: 11. And we dreamed a dream in one night, I and he; we dreamed each man according to the interpretation of his dream. 12. And *there was* there with us a young man, an Hebrew, servant to the captain of the guard; and we told him, and he interpreted to us our dreams; to each man according to his dream he did interpret. 13. And it came to pass, as he interpreted to us, so it was; me he restored unto mine office, and him he hanged. (Genesis 41:9–13)

So Pharaoh called for Joseph. To remember Pharaoh's troubling dreams, read Genesis 41:1–7. (Understand that *kine* means "a cow or a heifer.")

Read of the meeting between the pharaoh of Egypt and the prisoner, Joseph.

THE BIBLICAL PATH OF LIFE 96 LESSON 4

15. And Pharaoh said unto Joseph, I have dreamed a dream, and *there is* none that can interpret it: and I have heard say of thee, *that* thou canst understand a dream to interpret it. 16. And Joseph answered Pharaoh, saying, *It is* not in me: God shall give Pharaoh an answer of peace. … 25. And Joseph said unto Pharaoh, The dream of Pharaoh is one: God hath shewed Pharaoh what he is about to do. 26. The seven good kine *are* seven years; and the seven good ears *are* seven years: the dream *is* one. 27. And the seven thin and ill favoured kine that came up after them *are* seven years; and the seven empty ears blasted with the east wind shall be seven years of famine. 28. This *is* the thing which I have spoken unto Pharaoh: What God is about to do he sheweth unto Pharaoh. 29. Behold, there come seven years of great plenty throughout all the land of Egypt: 30. And there shall arise after them seven years of famine; and all the plenty shall be forgotten in the land of Egypt; and the famine shall consume the land; 31. And the plenty shall not be known in the land by reason of that famine following; for it *shall be* very grievous. 32. And for that the dream was doubled unto Pharaoh twice; *it is* because the thing *is* established by God, and God will shortly bring it to pass. (Genesis 41:15–16, 25–32).

Joseph told Pharaoh that God had given the dream and the answer. Joseph explained to Pharaoh that there would be seven years of plenty and then seven years of famine. Joseph then told Pharaoh what needed to be done.

LESSON 4 **97** THE BIBLICAL PATH OF LIFE

33. Now therefore let Pharaoh look out a man discreet and wise, and set him over the land of Egypt. 34. Let Pharaoh do *this*, and let him appoint officers over the land, and take up the fifth part of the land of Egypt in the seven plenteous years. 35. And let them gather all the food of those good years that come, and lay up corn under the hand of Pharaoh, and let them keep food in the cities. 36. And that food shall be for store to the land against the seven years of famine, which shall be in the land of Egypt; that the land perish not through the famine. (Genesis 41:33–36)

Joseph interpreting the Pharaoh's dream.

What did Pharaoh think of Joseph's words? "And the thing was good in the eyes of Pharaoh, and in the eyes of all his servants" (Genesis 41:37). Even the pharaoh of the land recognized God within this young man. "And Pharaoh said unto his servants, Can we find *such a one* as *this is*, a man in whom the Spirit of God *is*?" (Genesis 41:38).

THE BIBLICAL PATH OF LIFE 98 LESSON 4

What did Pharaoh do?

39. And Pharaoh said unto Joseph, Forasmuch as God hath shewed thee all this, *there is* none so discreet and wise as thou *art:* 40. Thou shalt be over my house, and according unto thy word shall all my people be ruled: only in the throne will I be greater than thou. 41. And Pharaoh said unto Joseph, See, I have set thee over all the land of Egypt. 42. And Pharaoh took off his ring from his hand, and put it upon Joseph's hand, and arrayed him in vestures of fine linen, and put a gold chain about his neck; 43. And he made him to ride in the second chariot which he had; and they cried before him, Bow the knee: and he made him ruler over all the land of Egypt. 44. And Pharaoh said unto Joseph, I *am* Pharaoh, and without thee shall no man lift up his hand or foot in all the land of Egypt. 45. And Pharaoh called Joseph's name Zaphnathpaaneah; and he gave him to wife Asenath the daughter of Potipherah priest of On. And Joseph went out over *all* the land of Egypt. 46. And Joseph *was* thirty years old when he stood before Pharaoh king of Egypt. And Joseph went out from the presence of Pharaoh, and went throughout all the land of Egypt. (Genesis 41:39–46)

Joseph was taken from being a prisoner in Egypt to the second in command of all of Egypt. The seven years of plenty followed by the seven years of famine came just as God had said (Genesis 41:47–56). See how far-reaching

LESSON 4   99   THE BIBLICAL PATH OF LIFE

this famine was—"And all countries came into Egypt to Joseph for to buy *corn*; because that the famine was *so* sore in all lands" (Genesis 41:57)—even in the land from which Joseph had been sold. "And Joseph's ten brethren went down to buy corn in Egypt" (Genesis 42:3).

Read Genesis 42–44 to remember the events of Joseph's brothers going to Egypt to buy food, not even recognizing that they were buying food from Joseph, the brother they had sold into slavery. But Joseph recognized them, and he had mercy upon them, for he still loved his brothers and had forgiven them long before. It is also here that we see the dreams Joseph had as a young man are fulfilled. When Joseph could no longer contain himself, he revealed himself to his brothers (Genesis 45:1–15). Joseph recognized that God was working in his life. "Now therefore be not grieved, nor angry with yourselves, that ye sold me hither: for God did send me before you to preserve life" (Genesis 45:5). The rest of that chapter reveals Joseph's invitation to come to Egypt to be with him, as well as Jacob's response when he heard his beloved son, Joseph, was still alive. Joseph was finally reunited with his father after many years (Genesis 46).

Once Jacob arrived in Egypt, Joseph introduced him to Pharaoh, securing the land of Goshen in which the family could reside. Joseph not only preserved the Egyptians' lives but provided for his family as well (Genesis 47).

In Genesis 48–49, Jacob blessed each of his sons, with Joseph's two boys receiving a double blessing. Especially notice the promise again of Jesus, who was to come. "The sceptre shall not depart from Judah, nor a lawgiver from between his feet, until Shiloh come; and unto him *shall* the gathering of the people *be*" (Genesis 49:10). Shiloh is the Messiah, Jesus, who was to come.

Read of the end of Joseph's life.

22. And Joseph dwelt in Egypt, he, and his father's house: and Joseph lived an hundred and ten years. 23. And

Joseph saw Ephraim's children of the third *generation*: the children also of Machir the son of Manasseh were brought up upon Joseph's knees. 24. And Joseph said unto his brethren, I die: and God will surely visit you, and bring you out of this land unto the land which he sware to Abraham, to Isaac, and to Jacob. 25. And Joseph took an oath of the children of Israel, saying, God will surely visit you, and ye shall carry up my bones from hence. 26. So Joseph died, *being* an hundred and ten years old: and they embalmed him, and he was put in a coffin in Egypt. (Genesis 50:22–26)

Joseph makes himself known to his brethren.

When Moses led the children of Israel out of Egypt, they carried the bones of Joseph with them, just as he had asked. "And Moses took the bones of Joseph with him: for he had straitly sworn the children of Israel, saying, God will surely visit you; and ye shall carry up my bones away hence with you" (Exodus 13:19).

LESSON 4   101   THE BIBLICAL PATH OF LIFE

5. Joseph, an Old Testament Picture of Christ

In the Old Testament, Joseph is one of the people we compare to a picture of Christ. Remember that when Joseph's brothers sold him into slavery, they meant it for evil. "But as for you, ye thought evil against me; *but* God meant it unto good, to bring to pass, as *it is* this day, to save much people alive" (Genesis 50:20). God sent His Son, Jesus, to save the world from their sin. He was the greatest gift ever given, but sinful man crucified him (evil against Him), and God took what man *intended* to be evil and delivered us from our sins by Jesus' death. Just as Joseph recognized that he was placed in a position to save the world from starvation, Jesus came to save the world from "the wages of sin … death" and instead gave us the "gift of God … eternal life through Jesus Christ our Lord" (Romans 6:23).

Joseph sold by his brethren.

JOSEPH AS A TYPE OF CHRIST
Compare Each Set of Scriptures (a and b)

The Beloved Son

1. The love of the father	a. Genesis 37:3	b. 2 Peter 1:17
2. The outward showing of honor	a. Genesis 37:3	b. Matthew 3:16–17
3. His father's messenger	a. Genesis 37:13–14	b. Luke 4:18

The Suffering Servant Who Was Rejected

1. The son who was hated	a. Genesis 37:4	b. John 15:24–25
2. Brothers who did not believe in him	a. Genesis 37:11	b. John 7:5
3. The plan to kill him	a. Genesis 37:18–21	b. Luke 4:24, 28–30
4. The son who was sold	a. Genesis 37:27–28	b. Matthew 27:9
5. The son who became a slave (servant)	a. Genesis 39:1	b. Philippians 2:7
6. The son's suffering:	a. Genesis 37:23–24, 42:21	b. Matthew 27:27–31
7. The death of the son:	a. Genesis 37:31–34, 44:20	b. John 19:30

The Hated Son Becomes the Savior

1. The son is exalted to the throne	a. Genesis 41:39–43	b. Philippians 2:9–11
2. Became savior of his people and the world	a. Genesis 41:55–57; Genesis 47:20, 25	b. Matthew 1:21, John 6:51
3. Made alive:	a. Genesis 45:26, 28	b. Romans 6:9, Revelation 1:18
4. Revealed before his brethren:	a. Genesis 45:3–4	b. Acts 1:3
5. Never one charge laid before him:	a. Genesis 41:38–39	b. 1 Peter 2:21–22, 1 John 3:5

LESSON 4 **103** THE BIBLICAL PATH OF LIFE

Reinforcement:

Joseph is an excellent example of enduring hatred and rejection from family members and still walking with God. When he was sold as a slave, Joseph still lived as an upright young man, choosing to do what was right in God's eyes. When falsely thrown into prison, God was still with Joseph, and Joseph honored God with his life.

In the past few lessons, we have seen where God promised to send One who would deliver a sinful people from their sins. In our last lesson, we saw once again the promise of a mighty Deliverer who would come (Genesis 28:14). Today we learned God promised to send "Shiloh" (Genesis 49:10). Better yet, we saw a picture of a mighty deliverer in Jacob's son, Joseph. God planned to send His Son, Jesus, from the beginning, and he constantly reminded mankind that He would come, sometimes giving them a verbal promise and other times a physical picture (like Joseph) to help them (and us today) understand. Jesus is God's greatest gift, for he came to save people from their sins. If you are leading a group, have your students think of ways they can tell others about the greatest gift ever. Remind them that just as Joseph saved people from starvation, Jesus came to save mankind from sin.

Closing:

It would be good to close with a short prayer reinforcing today's lesson. Always include any prayer requests you may have. *Today, pray for God to help us recognize that the gift of Jesus was promised from the beginning as the only way to be delivered from our sins. He was the greatest gift ever given. Pray we will remember the constant example of Joseph's faithfulness and strive to be as faithful to God.*

LESSON 4

Genesis 37–50
Joseph

Read Genesis 37–50. Complete the following.
Note: Jacob now has twelve sons and one daughter

1. Joseph was the eleventh-born son. Why did Jacob love him more? (Genesis 37:3) _____
_____ How did he show this? _____
_____

2. What were Joseph's two dreams? (Genesis 37:6–9) _____
_____
_____

3. How did Joseph's brothers feel about him after these dreams? (Genesis 37:5) _____

4. Because of this hatred, what did the oldest brothers plan? (Genesis 37:18–20) _____
_____

5. What changed their plans? (Genesis 37:25–28) _____
_____
_____

THE BIBLICAL PATH OF LIFE   LESSON 4

6. What did they lead their father to believe? (Genesis 37:31–35) _____

_____

What happened to Joseph? (37:36) _____

_____

Did God leave Joseph when he was away from his home and family? (Genesis 39:2) _____

7. When Joseph was falsely imprisoned, was God with him? (Genesis 39:20–21)

_____

8. While in prison, Pharaoh had a troubling dream. Joseph was called to interpret the dream. What was Joseph's answer? (Genesis 41:14–16) _____

_____

9. After Joseph tells of the seven years of plenty and then seven years of famine, what does Pharaoh do? (Genesis 41:39–44) _____

_____

10. How old was Joseph in Genesis 41:46? _____

11. How extensive was the famine? (Genesis 41:56–57) _____

12. From whom did Jacob's sons have to buy food? (Genesis 42:1–2, 6) _____

_____

13. Had Joseph forgiven his brothers? (Genesis 50:17–21) _____

_____

LESSON 4 **107** THE BIBLICAL PATH OF LIFE

Read Genesis 50:20.

Notice that Joseph recognized that God allowed the events in his life to bring him to the place to be able to save "much people alive." He was a savior to his people—any who would come to him. To us, Joseph is a picture in the Old Testament of Christ.

Answers:
1. He was the first son of Rachel; giving Joseph a coat of many colors;
2. he dreamed that his sheaf stood while his brother's sheaves made obeisance to his; he dreamed the sun, moon, and eleven stars made obeisance to him;
3. they hated him yet the more;
4. to kill Joseph, cast him into a pit, and then say an evil beast devoured him;
5. they saw a company coming from Egypt and decided to make a profit by selling him;
6. that an evil beast had devoured Joseph because of the blood on his coat; Joseph was sold to Potiphar; no;
7. yes;
8. God would give the answer of peace;
9. Pharaoh made Joseph ruler over all the land of Egypt;
10. thirty years old;
11. over all the face of the earth;
12. Joseph;
13. yes

EXODUS 1–18
FROM EGYPT THROUGH THE WILDERNESS

LESSON 5

Key Verse

And I will take you to me for a people, and I will be to you a God: and ye shall know that I am the LORD your God …

—EXODUS 6:7

Key Verse Thought: After reading the key verse, make sure you understand the importance of recognizing God in our lives. He is to be our God, and we are to be His people.

Emphasis: To recognize is that God revealed Himself to His people in the Old Testament, and He will do the same for His people today.

Lesson Summary: Between Genesis and Exodus, God's people grew into a nation numbering around two to three million people. At least four hundred years had passed since they entered into Egypt. We see the mighty deliverance of God's people from a land of bondage (Egypt). We see the power of God revealed through this time of exodus. The passing through the Red Sea prevented their return to the land of bondage. The old way of life was left behind forever.

But of all of these events, the most important is that God revealed Himself to His people. He reminded them that He was their God, and that they were His people (remember today's key verse). He showed them that He was their God through the ten plagues and the mighty deliverance from bondage.

Suggested Bible Reading to Prepare for This Lesson

- Monday: **Exodus 1–3**
- Tuesday: **Exodus 4–6**
- Wednesday: **Exodus 7–9**
- Thursday: **Exodus 10–12**
- Friday: **Exodus 13–15**
- Saturday: **Exodus 16–18**

Exodus 1–18:
From Egypt through the Wilderness

1 Moses' birth through God's call—Exodus 1–4

- **Chapter 1:** Pharaoh's decree that all male babies be killed
- **Chapter 2:** Moses is born; kills an Egyptian, flees, and marries. The people cry out from bondage.
- **Chapter 3:** Moses is called (the burning bush). God revealed as I Am.
- **Chapter 4:** Aaron to assist Moses; Zipporah saves Moses' life, and Moses returns to Egypt.

2 God revealed to His people and then to Pharaoh—Exodus 5–12

- **Chapter 5:** Moses and Aaron before Pharaoh; Israelites to do more work without straw.
- **Chapter 6:** God to be revealed to the people, not just individuals (vs. 3–8), genealogy
- **Chapter 7:** Rod to serpent; water to blood (first plague)
- **Chapter 8:** Frogs (second plague), lice (third plague), flies (fourth plague)
- **Chapter 9:** Cattle die (fifth plague), ashes, boils (sixth plague), thunder, hail, and fire (seventh plague)

THE BIBLICAL PATH OF LIFE **112** LESSON 5

- **Chapter 10:** Locusts (eighth plague), darkness for three days (ninth plague)
- **Chapter 11:** Israelites told to spoil the Egyptians and told of the tenth plague
- **Chapter 12:** Passover instituted, death of firstborn (tenth plague), spoiled Egyptians, leave Egypt

3 God's presence with His people—Exodus 13–15:1–21

- **Chapter 13:** Consecration of firstborn, pillar of a cloud by day and a pillar of fire by night
- **Chapter 14:** Pharaoh pursued Israelites; crossing of Red Sea
- **Chapter 15:** 1–21: Song of Moses

4 God provides for his own—Exodus 15:22–18

- **Chapter 15:22–27:** Tree in the bitter water
- **Chapter 16:** Manna in the morning; quail in the evening
- **Chapter 17:** Moses to smite the rock for water; battle with Amalek where Moses' arms are raised
- **Chapter 18:** Jethro (Moses' father-in-law) comes; judges are appointed

1. Moses birth through God's call
—Exodus 1–4

If you remember, Joseph was a ruler in the land of Egypt, second only to Pharaoh. When the famine came upon the land, he was reunited with his family. He then moved them to Egypt with him to the land of Goshen. About 350 years pass before we pick up the history of the Israelites. We find that there is a new king, a pharaoh who didn't know Joseph. "Now there arose up a new king over Egypt, which knew not Joseph" (Exodus 1:8). He realized that there were more Israelites now than Egyptians, so they made the Israelites their slaves. But the people multiplied. So he ordered all male children to be killed. Moses' mother, Jochebed, made a basket and saved him by the water. "1. And there went a man of the house of Levi, and took *to wife* a daughter of Levi. 2. And the woman conceived, and bare a son: and when she saw him that he *was a* goodly *child*, she hid him three months. 3. And when she could not longer hide him, she took for him an ark of bulrushes, and daubed it with slime and with pitch, and put the child therein; and she laid it in the flags by the river's brink. 4. And his sister stood afar off, to wit what would be done to him" (Exodus 2:1–4).

Here we see God's justice in action. Jochebed's faithfulness is rewarded as Miriam offers to find a nurse for the baby.

> 5. And the daughter of Pharaoh came down to wash *herself* at the river; and her maidens walked along by the river's side; and when she saw the ark among the flags, she sent her maid to fetch it. 6. And when she had opened it, she

saw the child: and, behold, the babe wept. And she had compassion on him, and said, This *is one* of the Hebrews' children. 7. Then said his sister to Pharaoh's daughter, Shall I go and call to thee a nurse of the Hebrew women, that she may nurse the child for thee? 8. And Pharaoh's daughter said to her, Go. And the maid went and called the child's mother. 9. And Pharaoh's daughter said unto her, Take this child away, and nurse it for me, and I will give *thee* thy wages. And the woman took the child, and nursed it. 10. And the child grew, and she brought him unto Pharaoh's daughter, and he became her son. And she called his name Moses: and she said, Because I drew him out of the water. (Exodus 2:5–10)

Pharaoh's daughter finding baby Moses

Moses' own mother got to nurse her baby and ground him in his heritage. Moses then grew up in Pharaoh's palace.

But Moses knew his people were slaves. He tried to help his people in his way; he killed an Egyptian and then fled.

11. And it came to pass in those days, when Moses was grown, that he went out unto his brethren, and looked on their burdens: and he spied an Egyptian smiting an Hebrew, one of his brethren. 12. And he looked this way and that way, and when he saw that *there was* no man, he slew the

LESSON 5 115 THE BIBLICAL PATH OF LIFE

Egyptian, and hid him in the sand. 13. And when he went out the second day, behold, two men of the Hebrews strove together: and he said to him that did the wrong, Wherefore smitest thou thy fellow? 14. And he said, Who made thee a prince and a judge over us? intendest thou to kill me, as thou killedst the Egyptian? And Moses feared, and said, Surely this thing is known. 15. Now when Pharaoh heard this thing, he sought to slay Moses. But Moses fled from the face of Pharaoh, and dwelt in the land of Midian: and he sat down by a well. (Exodus 2:11–15)

But God remembered his people. "23. And it came to pass in process of time, that the king of Egypt died: and the children of Israel sighed by reason of the bondage, and they cried, and their cry came up unto God by reason of the bondage. 24. And God heard their groaning, and God remembered his covenant with Abraham, with Isaac, and with Jacob. 25. And God looked upon the children of Israel, and God had respect unto them" (Exodus 2:23–25).

Moses married, had a son, and raised sheep in the land of Midian. While he was tending his sheep, he saw a strange sight and turned to see it—a bush was burning but not being consumed. Then God called him.

1. Now Moses kept the flock of Jethro his father in law, the priest of Midian: and he led the flock to the backside of the desert, and came to the mountain of God, *even* to Horeb. 2. And the angel of the LORD appeared unto him in a flame of fire out of the midst of a bush: and he looked, and, behold, the bush burned with fire, and the bush *was* not consumed. 3. And Moses said, I will now turn aside,

and see this great sight, why the bush is not burnt. 4. And when the LORD saw that he turned aside to see, God called unto him out of the midst of the bush, and said, Moses, Moses. And he said, Here *am* I. (Exodus 3:1–4)

God revealed himself to Moses. "6. Moreover he said, I *am* the God of thy father, the God of Abraham, the God of Isaac, and the God of Jacob. And Moses hid his face; for he was afraid to look upon God … 14. And God said unto Moses, I AM THAT I AM: and he said, Thus shalt thou say unto the children of Israel, I AM hath sent me unto you" (Exodus 3:6, 14). God had a plan for Moses to deliver His people from bondage (read Exodus 3:7–22). God would speak to Moses, and Moses would speak God's words to Aaron. Aaron would become Moses' voice. "And he shall be thy spokesman unto the people: and he shall be, even he shall be to thee instead of a mouth, and thou shalt be to him instead of God" (Exodus 4:16).

Focus on God's call to Moses to lead His people. Even though Moses was quite reluctant, thinking himself inadequate, God still used him. God will use those who are willing to be used by Him. God wants to be actively involved in His people's lives.

God called Moses while he was about his daily life. Also take note that when God called Moses, Moses responded to that call, even though he didn't think he could do it. God provided the means for him to accomplish the task laid out before him. Aaron, his brother, would be his voice, and God provided Moses with signs to show Pharaoh.

LESSON 5   117   THE BIBLICAL PATH OF LIFE

2. God revealed to His people and then to Pharaoh —Exodus 5–12

Moses and Aaron appeared before Pharaoh and told him, "Thus saith the LORD God of Israel, Let my people go …" (Exodus 5:1). Pharaoh's response? "…I know not the LORD, neither will I let Israel go" (Exodus 5:2).

God then revealed himself to His people, not just an individual as in the past (see key verse). God reminded them of the covenant He had established with their forefathers. He wanted them to know that He would honor that covenant with them, His chosen people (Exodus 6:2–8). The people did not listen to God's words because of their bondage (Exodus 6:9). So God sent Moses to Pharaoh. God would reveal himself mightily to Pharaoh. Exodus 7–12 tell of the ten plagues (the last one being the Passover). The people then spoil Egypt, pack up, and then leave after 430 years in the land of Egypt (Exodus 12:20), carrying the bones of Joseph with them (Exodus 13:19).

Moses and Aaron Appear before Pharaoh.

THE TEN PLAGUES

1. Rod to serpent; water to blood
2. Frogs
3. Lice
4. Flies
5. Cattle die
6. Ashes, boils
7. Thunder, hail, and fire
8. Locusts
9. Darkness for three days
10. Passover angel and death of firstborn

A Deeper Path:

Focus mainly on the fact that God revealed himself to His people—His chosen people. He reminded them of that covenant He had made with Abraham, Isaac, and Jacob (God had not forgotten). God revealed to His people that he wanted to have a relationship with them (see Exodus 6:6–8), just as he wants to have a relationship with us today. "16b. ... for ye are the temple of the living God; as God hath said, I will dwell in them, and walk in them; and I will be their God, and they shall be my people. 17. Wherefore come out from among them, and be ye separate, saith the Lord, and touch not the unclean thing; and I will receive you, 18. And will be a Father unto you, and ye shall be my sons and daughters, saith the Lord Almighty" (2 Corinthians 6:16b–18).

3. God's presence with His people
—Exodus 13–15:1–21

God promised to be with His people. He made Himself known to them in a pillar of cloud by day and a pillar of fire by night. When the pillar moved, they were to follow. "20. And they took their journey from Succoth, and encamped in Etham, in the edge of the wilderness. 21. And the LORD went before them by day in a pillar of a cloud, to lead them the way; and by night in a pillar of fire, to give them light; to go by day and night: 22. He took not away the pillar of the cloud by day, nor the pillar of fire by night, from before the people" (Exodus 13:20–22).

After they left Egypt, Pharaoh had another change of heart. He pursued them with all of his horses, chariots, horsemen, and his army. They overtook the Israelites as they were encamped by the sea.

4. And I will harden Pharaoh's heart, that he shall follow after them; and I will be honoured upon Pharaoh, and upon all his host; that the Egyptians may know that I *am* the LORD. And they did so. 5. And it was told the king of Egypt that the people fled: and the heart of Pharaoh and of his servants was turned against the people, and they said, Why have we done this, that we have let Israel go from serving us? 6. And he made ready his chariot, and took his people with him: 7. And he took six hundred chosen chariots, and all the chariots of Egypt, and captains over every one of them. 8. And the LORD

hardened the heart of Pharaoh king of Egypt, and he pursued after the children of Israel: and the children of Israel went out with an high hand. 9. But the Egyptians pursued after them, all the horses *and* chariots of Pharaoh, and his horsemen, and his army, and overtook them encamping by the sea, beside Pihahiroth, before Baalzephon. (Exodus 14:4–9)

The people were scared, but Moses encouraged them. "13. And Moses said unto the people, Fear ye not, stand still, and see the salvation of the LORD, which he will shew to you to day: for the Egyptians whom ye have seen to day, ye shall see them again no more for ever. 14. The LORD shall fight for you, and ye shall hold your peace" (Exodus 14:13–14). The pillar of the cloud stood behind them, between their camp and the Egyptian army, making the Egyptian camp dark and the Israelites' camp light. Moses held his rod over the Red Sea, and it parted. All of the Israelites passed through on dry ground while the Red Sea was held up on each side. The Egyptian army pursued them into the dry bed of the sea. God caused the wheels to fall off their chariots, and then the waters came upon them, and all of Pharaoh's army drowned (read Exodus 14:23–31 to remember these events). God had eliminated the threat—completely.

Understand that when we belong to Jesus, He wants us to follow him daily. "And he said to *them* all, If any *man* will come after me, let him deny himself, and take up his cross daily, and follow me" (Luke 9:23). He promised to always be with us and take care of us. "5b. … for he hath said, I will never leave thee, nor forsake thee. So that we may boldly say, The Lord *is* my helper, and I will not fear what man shall do unto me" (Hebrews 13:5b-6).

4. God provides for his own
—Exodus 15:22–18

After Moses praised God in song for the mighty deliverance from Pharaoh's army, the people came to a place where there was bitter water. The people began to murmur. Moses called to God and was told to cast a tree into the water, and the water was good to drink (read Exodus 15). When they murmured about food, God then provided them manna each morning and quail that evening (read Exodus 16). They camped in another place, and there was no water. Moses entreated God, saying the people would stone him if they did not get water. God gave Moses directions to strike a rock with his rod, and water would come out of it (read Exodus 17:1–7). Then Amalek came and fought against Israel. Moses sent Joshua to choose men to fight. Moses stood on the hill. As long as Moses held up his hands, they prevailed in battle. But when Moses' arms began to go down, they began to lose the battle. Two men held up Moses' arms until the battle was won (read Exodus 17:8–16).

Jethro (Moses' father-in-law) came and stayed with the Israelites after he heard what God had done for His people, and he believed (read Exodus 18:1–12). Jethro gave Moses advice, that he should appoint judges to help Moses judge the people in all their matters.

God led them into the wilderness, but He provided for their every need—food, water, a cloud by day (for shade during the heat of the day), and a pillar of fire at night (to provide them light). God still provides for His own today. "But my God shall supply all your need according to his riches in glory by Christ Jesus" (Philippians 4:19). Not only did God provide for their needs, but He was with them in that provision. Another way

THE BIBLICAL PATH OF LIFE **122** LESSON 5

He revealed himself to His people was by meeting their spiritual needs (which they didn't realize they needed) as well as their physical needs. In the New Testament we get an extra insight. "And did all drink the same spiritual drink: for they drank of that spiritual Rock that followed them: and that Rock was Christ" (1 Corinthians 10:4). Jesus was with them, even in the wilderness. (Also see John 4:10; 7:38.)

Moses strikes the rock, and God gave them water.

Reinforcement:

Be encouraged to not only remember the story of Moses, the ten plagues, the crossing of the Red Sea, and the entering into the wilderness but that God was with them. He provided their every need. He made Himself known to His people, just as He will do for His people today.

Have you considered God's provision for His people? Do you realize when we ask Jesus in our hearts, we are no longer our own? We belong to God because we have been bought with a price. "19. What? know ye not that your body is the temple of the Holy Ghost which is in you, which ye have of God, and ye are not your own? 20. For ye are bought with a price: therefore glorify God in your body, and in your spirit, which are God's" (1 Corinthians 6:19–20). We can no longer please ourselves. Our job is to please God with every part of our lives.

Closing:

It would be good to close with a short prayer reinforcing today's lesson. Always include any prayer requests you may have. *Today, pray for God to help us to realize that we belong to Him and to hear Him when He calls upon us. Pray we will remember to live our lives pleasing Him. Thank God for always providing for our needs.*

LESSON 5

Exodus 1–18
From Egypt through the Wilderness

Read Exodus 1–18. Complete the following.

1. About 350 years passed after Joseph moved his family into the land of Egypt with a new pharaoh who did not know Joseph. What did the new pharaoh do? (Exodus 1:8–11) _____
_____
_____

2. When the people multiplied, what did Pharaoh command? (Exodus 1:22) _____

3. How did one woman save her son? (Exodus 2:1–4) _____
_____

4. Where was that son raised, and what was his name? (Exodus 2:5–10) _____

5. Why did Moses flee Egypt? (Exodus 2:11–15) _____
_____
_____

LESSON 5   125   THE BIBLICAL PATH OF LIFE

6. While tending his flock in Midian, what did Moses see? (Exodus 3:1–3) _____

Who called Moses? (Exodus 3:4–6) _____

What did God want Moses to do? (Exodus 3:7–10) _____

_____

7. What did Moses say, and who did God send with him? (Exodus 4:10–17) _____

_____

> **NOTE:** God called Moses while he was about his daily life, and Moses responded to that call.

8. What did Moses and Aaron ask Pharaoh? (Exodus 5:1) _____
_____

9. What was Pharaoh's response? (Exodus 5:2) _____
_____

10. God revealed Himself to His people. What did He tell them? (Exodus 6:2–8) _____
_____
_____

11. How did God lead the people? (Exodus 13:20–22) _____
_____

12. Pharaoh changed his mind after the people left. What did he do? (Exodus 14:5–9) _____

What did Moses say when they saw Pharaoh's army? (Exodus 14:13–14)_____

_____

_____

13. What did the people do? (Exodus 14:21–22) _____

_____

14. What happened to the Egyptian army? (Exodus 14:23–28) _____

_____

15. What did the people do shortly after this mighty deliverance? (Exodus 16:2–3)

_____

_____

16. How did God provide for them? (Exodus 16:4)_____

_____

17. What did the people ask for in the wilderness of Sin? (Exodus 17:1–3)_____

_____

_____

18. What did God tell Moses to do? (Exodus 17:4–6) _____

_____

_____

LESSON 5 **127** THE BIBLICAL PATH OF LIFE

19. What unusual thing happened in the battle with Amalek? (Exodus 17:11) _____
_____ Did they win the battle? (Exodus 17:13) _____

20. How did Moses' father-in-law, Jethro, respond when he heard what God had done for the Israelites? (Exodus 18:8–11) _____
_____

Remember *Each person has a choice when he or she hears about God—either receive or reject.*

Answers:
1. Set taskmasters over them and caused them to afflict them and build treasure cities
2. Cast the sons in the river
3. Put him into the river in an ark covered with slime and pitch
4. Pharaoh's house, Moses
5. He killed an Egyptian
6. A bush that burned but wasn't consumed; God; bring the people of Israel out of Egypt
7. He was slow of speech; Aaron
8. The Lord said to let My people go
9. I know not the LORD, neither will I let Israel go
10. God reminded them of the covenant He had established with their forefathers. God wanted them to know that He would honor that covenant with them, His chosen people
11. Pillar of cloud by day and pillar of fire by night
12. All of the Egyptians horses, chariots, and the army pursued them; fear not, stand still, and see the salvation of the Lord for they would see the Egyptian army no more
13. Crossed in the midst of the Red Sea on dry land
14. They pursued, the waters came again and drowned them
15. Murmured and complained
16. He rained bread (manna) from heaven for them to gather
17. Water
18. Take his rod and smite the rock
19. When Moses hands were held up, they prevailed in battle; yes
20. He rejoiced and believed the Lord is greater than all gods

THE BIBLICAL PATH OF LIFE **128** LESSON 5

EXODUS 19–40
GOD REVEALED

LESSON 6

Key Verse

Now therefore, if ye will obey my voice indeed, and keep my covenant, then ye shall be a peculiar treasure unto me above all people: for all the earth is mine.

—EXODUS 19:5

Key Verse Thought: In today's key verse, "peculiar treasure" refers to the people of Israel as God's private possession because He chose them, delivered them from Egyptian bondage, and shaped them into what He wanted them to be (called *jewels* in Malachi 3:17). Just as we feel treasures and jewels are special and important, God considers His people His special treasure or jewel. Today we understand that Christians are a "peculiar treasure" to God (Titus 2:14; 1 Peter 2:9). We are very special and important to Him.

Emphasis: Understand that Christians are to be a peculiar treasure to God. "For ye are bought with a price: therefore glorify God in your body, and in your spirit, which are God's" (1 Corinthians 6:20).

THE BIBLICAL PATH OF LIFE 130 LESSON 6

Lesson Summary: God proved His power when He delivered His people from bondage in Egypt. He had chosen them to be a special people to Him. He now proves His holiness by commanding His people to be holy. He gave them laws so they could obey Him. He sent His Angel (Jesus) to go before them and lead them. God revealed Jesus through the tabernacle and its furnishings. God even gave them someone talented to build it and the implements to be placed inside. In spite of all of this, they forgot God, worshiping an idol. Moses prayed for them. God still left His Angel (Jesus) with them to lead them. When they finished the tabernacle and set it up, God came down in a cloud of glory and dwelt among His people.

Suggested Bible Reading to Prepare for This Lesson

- Monday: **Exodus 19–22**
- Tuesday: **Exodus 23–26**
- Wednesday: **Exodus 27–30**
- Thursday: **Exodus 31–34**
- Friday: **Exodus 35–37**
- Saturday: **Exodus 38–40**

LESSON 6 131 THE BIBLICAL PATH OF LIFE

Exodus 19–40: God Revealed

1 **God's people are a "peculiar treasure" (Exodus 19–20).**

- God chose them to be special to Him: (1) the relationship, (2) the role, (3) the lifestyle (Exodus 19:1–8).
- God wanted to meet with His people at the foot of the mount (Exodus 19:9–24).
- Moses to tell the people God's commands, the Ten Commandments (Exodus 19:25–20:17).
- The people are to fear God (Exodus 20:18–21).

2 **God will take care of His people (Exodus 23:20–33; 24:3–11).**

- An angel before them, and they are to serve God only (Exodus 23:20–25).
- The people promise to obey God's Word (Exodus 24:3, 7).
- After commitment, Moses and the seventy elders see God, under His feet (Exodus 24:9–11). See the following verses: John 1:18; Ezekiel 1:26–28 (Ezekiel's vision of the throne of God); Revelation 4:2–3 (describes God's throne).

THE BIBLICAL PATH OF LIFE **132** LESSON 6

3 **God commands the building of the tabernacle and its implements (Exodus 25–31).**

- How to build the tabernacle and its implements (Exodus 25–30).
- God appoints a man to lead in building (Exodus 31:1–11).

4 **The people forget God (Exodus 32).**

- Aaron makes a golden calf, and the people worship it (Exodus 32:1–6).
- God sees and wants to destroy them (Exodus 32:7–10), but Moses intercedes (Exodus 32:11–14).
- Moses sees the people and calls for a separation (Exodus 32:19–29).
- Moses pleads for forgiveness for the people (Exodus 32:30–32).
- God promises to lead the people; His angel shall go before them (Exodus 32:34–35).

5 **They are reminded of the promise, and God with His people (Exodus 33 and 40).**

- Promise made to Abraham, Isaac, and Jacob reconfirmed (Exodus 33:1–3).
- The tabernacle is set up (Exodus 40:17, 33).
- God's presence fills the tabernacle (Exodus 40:34–38).

LESSON 6 THE BIBLICAL PATH OF LIFE

1. God's people are a "peculiar treasure"
(Exodus 19–20).

God had showed Himself mightily to His people. There is a pause here as God gave direction to Moses to relay to the people. Now that the people had seen God reveal Himself, they needed to understand the relationship.

4. Ye have seen what I did unto the Egyptians, and *how* I bare you on eagles' wings, and brought you unto myself. 5. Now therefore, if ye will obey my voice indeed, and keep my covenant, then ye shall be a peculiar treasure unto me above all people: for all the earth *is* mine: 6. And ye shall be unto me a kingdom of priests, and an holy nation. These *are* the words which thou shalt speak unto the children of Israel. 7. And Moses came and called for the elders of the people, and laid before their faces all these words which the LORD commanded him. 8. And all the people answered together, and said, All that the LORD hath spoken we will do. And Moses returned the words of the people unto the LORD. 9. And the LORD said unto Moses, Lo, I come unto thee in a thick cloud, that the people may hear when I speak with thee, and believe thee for ever. And Moses told the words of the people unto the LORD. (Exodus 19:4–9)

God reminded them of what He had done (delivered them mightily). He then told them that if they would obey His voice and keep His covenant, they would be a "peculiar treasure" to Him, above all people. They would be so special to Him that they would constantly be under His watch care. He would guard and protect them as one would a special treasure. A relationship was to be established; this was to be the best part. They were allowed the privilege of having a covenant relationship with God Himself. We then see the role the people are to perform; that is to be a kingdom of priests. As such, they had immediate access to God. No other people in the world could claim this. By having a relationship with God, they placed themselves under His authority; to obey Him and His Word.

To become a holy nation required a change in lifestyle. They had to obey God's commands (and no longer live as they once did). When the people heard what God required of them, they committed themselves to do it. "7. And Moses came and called for the elders of the people, and laid before their faces all these words which the LORD commanded him. 8. And all the people answered together, and said, All that the LORD hath spoken we will do. And Moses returned the words of the people unto the LORD" (Exodus 19:7–8).

Moses descends from Mount Sinai.

LESSON 6 **135** THE BIBLICAL PATH OF LIFE

God had called for the people to meet at the foot of His mountain so that He could speak to Moses where the people could hear.

God had called the people to meet at the foot of His mountain.

10. And the LORD said unto Moses, Go unto the people, and sanctify them to day and to morrow, and let them wash their clothes, 11. And be ready against the third day: for the third day the LORD will come down in the sight of all the people upon mount Sinai. 12. And thou shalt set bounds unto the people round about, saying, Take heed to yourselves, *that ye* go *not* up into the mount, or touch the border of it: whosoever toucheth the mount shall be surely put to death: 13. There shall not an hand touch it, but he shall surely be stoned, or shot through; *whether it be* beast or man, it shall not live: when the trumpet soundeth long, they shall come up to the mount. 14. And Moses went down from the mount unto the people, and sanctified the people; and they washed their clothes. 15. And he said unto the people, Be ready against the third day: come not at *your* wives. (Exodus 19:10–15).

THE BIBLICAL PATH OF LIFE 136 LESSON 6

On the third day, there was thunder and lightning and a thick cloud upon the mount. There also was the "voice of the trumpet exceeding loud." This terrified the people, yet they came out to meet God. Then there was smoke upon the mount because the Lord descended upon it in fire—"And mount Sinai was altogether on a smoke, because the LORD descended upon it in fire: and the smoke thereof ascended as the smoke of a furnace, and the whole mount quaked greatly" (Exodus 19:18)—and the whole mount quaked greatly. Moses had set a boundary around the mount so that the people would not go up on it because God had commanded it. "And Moses said unto the LORD, The people cannot come up to mount Sinai: for thou chargedst us, saying, Set bounds about the mount, and sanctify it" (Exodus 19:23). While the trumpet still sounded, long and loud, Moses spoke to God, and God answered him by a voice. God then told Moses to go down and then come up the mount without the people.

Exodus 20 records the Ten Commandments that God speaks. See that God Himself gave these commands to the people. "And God spake all these words, saying" (Exodus 20:1). If you are a group leader, review these commandments with your class (found in Exodus 20:1–17). Help them understand these commands. Notice that the first four deal with our relationship with God. The following six deal with our relationship with other people. First our relationship must be right with God, and then we can have a proper relationship with others. By giving the people these commands, they could recognize the condition of man because of sin. It still took faith (as Abraham showed, walking perfect, sincere, and upright before God) to do what God commanded.

After the commandments were given, the people removed themselves from the mountain and told Moses to speak to them, and they would hear. They were afraid to hear God speak. "18. And all the people saw the thunderings,

LESSON 6 137 THE BIBLICAL PATH OF LIFE

and the lightnings, and the noise of the trumpet, and the mountain smoking: and when the people saw *it*, they removed, and stood afar off. 19. And they said unto Moses, Speak thou with us, and we will hear: but let not God speak with us, lest we die" (Exodus 20:18–19). Notice that is exactly the response God wanted from his people—fear "that ye sin not."

"And Moses said unto the people, Fear not: for God is come to prove you, and that his fear may be before your faces, that ye sin not" (Exodus 20:20). Moses drew near and heard the rest of the words God had for his people.

Most people have heard the Ten Commandments so many times that they *think* they already know them. See them in a new light today. Emphasize that the first four deal with our relationship with God, followed by the six that deal with our relationship with other people. Then compare this knowledge with Matthew 22:36–39, as follows: "36. Master, which is the great commandment in the law? 37. Jesus said unto him, Thou shalt love the Lord thy God with all thy heart, and with all thy soul, and with all thy mind. 38. This is the first and great commandment. 39. And the second is like unto it, Thou shalt love thy neighbour as thyself."

Jesus also broke it down into two areas: love God right; then love mankind right. If the "religious people" (Sadducees and Pharisees) could not accept this, they couldn't be right with God. Jesus went on to tell them the importance of understanding this. "On these two commandments hang all the law and the prophets" (Matthew 22:40).

2. God will take care of His people
(Exodus 23:20–33; 24:3–11)

God promised to send "an Angel" to go before them. "Behold, I send an Angel before thee, to keep thee in the way, and to bring thee into the place which I have prepared" (Exodus 23:20). If you remember, "the angel of the Lord appeared to Moses in a flame of fire out of the midst of the bush" (Exodus 3:2). It goes on to tell us that God spoke to him from that bush. We see that angel again in Exodus 14:19, as it stood behind the Israelites, protecting them from the Egyptian army. The angel in each of these places (and more) is considered the preincarnate Christ (Jesus before he was born as a man on the earth). God told them to obey that "Angel's" voice. God's name is in him. "Beware of him, and obey his voice, provoke him not; for he will not pardon your transgressions: for my name is in him" (Exodus 23:21). Also, see in the New Testament where Jesus is speaking when he said "that the

God spoke with Moses from a bush.

LESSON 6 139 THE BIBLICAL PATH OF LIFE

Father is in me, and I in him" (John 10:38b). When God promised to send that "Angel" (Exodus 23:20), He was to keep them and lead them to the place God prepared for His people (the Promised Land). As long as they obeyed His voice and did all He commanded them, God promised to be an enemy to their enemies and an adversary to their adversaries. "But if thou shalt indeed obey his voice, and do all that I speak; then I will be an enemy unto thine enemies, and an adversary unto thine adversaries" (Exodus 23:22). God commanded them to not bow to false gods or serve them, nor to do after their works. They were to completely remove them and any semblance of them when they entered the land God promised them. They were reminded to serve God and Him only.

When the people heard the words of the Lord, they answered with one voice—they would do it all. Moses then wrote it down and read the book of the covenant to the people, and they responded again in affirmation. They would do all that the Lord said for them to do. They made a promise.

The people said they would do all that the Lord said for them to do.

Next, in Exodus 24, we see Moses; Aaron; his two sons, Nadab and Abihu, and seventy of the elders allowed to go up the mount. There, God revealed something special to them. They were allowed to see the divine presence of God in heaven. God gave them this special time and did nothing harmful to them (remember in Exodus 19:12, 21, the people were warned not to go up onto the mount lest they perish). Ezekiel later saw a similar vision (Ezekiel 1:26–28).

THE BIBLICAL PATH OF LIFE 140 LESSON 6

3. God commands the building of the tabernacle and its implements

(Exodus 25–31)

Moses went back up the mount. Read Exodus 24:15–18 to see what the people saw when this happened. Notice it tells us that Moses was up there for forty days and forty nights. Keep this information in mind for the events that transpire later.

God tells Moses specific details about the tabernacle and its implements. One important thing to understand is that everything about it was to show them Jesus. Each piece that was to go into the tabernacle represented Christ. Read through Exodus 25–31 to see the intricate details they were to follow. God is a God of detail. He sees the smallest and wants it just right (even in our hearts and lives). He knows all. Just looking at the specifications He wanted for the

The Tabernacle in the Wilderness.

LESSON 6 141 THE BIBLICAL PATH OF LIFE

earthly implements in the tabernacle (and the tabernacle itself) should just give us a glimpse into how important even the small things are to God. We must take this into consideration as we live our lives before God. Remember: we are the temple of the living God. "… for ye are the temple of the living God; as God hath said, I will dwell in them, and walk in *them*; and I will be their God, and they shall be my people" (2 Corinthians 6:16b).

It is especially interesting to note that God gave them a special person to make these things. He was to lead them in this "building project." God had filled this man (Bezaleel) with the "spirit of God" and gifted him with the ability to do all that God wanted done. He even gave this man others to help him. God never asks His people to do anything that He won't provide the way and the people to do it. We just have to be willing to be used by God (just as Bezaleel and his helpers were).

There is a great parallel in the implements of the tabernacle to Jesus in the book of John.

The implements for the tabernacle were as follows:

1. **Brazen altar—a blood sacrifice for atonement (John 1:29)**
2. **Brazen laver—regeneration (spiritual renewal) by washing (John 3:3, 5; Titus 3:5–6)**
3. **Table of shewbread—spiritual nourishment (John 6:35, 44–48)**
4. **Golden candlestick—spiritual enlightenment (John 8:12; 9:5)**
5. **Altar of incense—sweet odor; prayers of the saints (John 14:13–14; Revelation 5:8; 8:3–4)**
6. **The ark of the covenant (and mercy seat where the blood was sprinkled)—access because of a covenant; held covenant inside (John 20:17—access to God through Jesus; and Romans 3:25)**

4. The people forget God
(Exodus 32)

Aaron fashioned a golden calf for the people to worship in the wilderness. This is a very familiar Bible story, but become familiar with facts about it that you may not know or remember.

The people last saw Moses when he went up on the mount to talk with God (Exodus 24:15–18). "And when the people saw that Moses delayed to come down out of the mount, the people gathered themselves together unto Aaron, and said unto him, Up, make us gods, which shall go before us; for *as for* this Moses, the man that brought us up out of the land of Egypt, we wot not what is become of him" (Exodus 32:1). The people had lost hope that Moses would return. They demanded that Aaron make them gods to worship. Notice how quickly the people forgot God. If we, as Christians, do not keep in constant communication with God and keep Him ever before us, we too will forget God and replace Him with other "gods" of our own. When Aaron finished fashioning the calf from all of the people's earrings, he presented it as their god and proceeded to worship it. God saw and wanted to destroy His people.

> 7. And the LORD said unto Moses, Go, get thee down; for thy people, which thou broughtest out of the land of Egypt, have corrupted *themselves*: 8. They have turned aside quickly out of the way which I commanded them: they have made them a molten calf, and have worshipped it, and have sacrificed thereunto, and said, These *be* thy

LESSON 6 **143** THE BIBLICAL PATH OF LIFE

gods, O Israel, which have brought thee up out of the land of Egypt. 9. And the LORD said unto Moses, I have seen this people, and, behold, it is a stiffnecked people: 10. Now therefore let me alone, that my wrath may wax hot against them, and that I may consume them: and I will make of thee a great nation. (Exodus 32:7–10)

Moses interceded on their behalf.

11. And Moses besought the LORD his God, and said, LORD, why doth thy wrath wax hot against thy people, which thou hast brought forth out of the land of Egypt with great power, and with a mighty hand? 12. Wherefore should the Egyptians speak, and say, For mischief did he bring them out, to slay them in the mountains, and to consume them from the face of the earth? Turn from thy fierce wrath, and repent of this evil against thy people. 13. Remember Abraham, Isaac, and Israel, thy servants, to whom thou swarest by thine own self, and saidst unto them, I will multiply your seed as the stars of heaven, and all this land that I have spoken of will I give unto your seed, and they shall inherit *it* for ever. (Exodus 32:11–13)

He reminded God of the covenant with His people and the witness it would be to the nations for God to forsake His own people. We see God turn from the evil he had planned. "And the LORD repented of the evil which he thought to do unto his people" (Exodus 32:14). The people were spared.

THE BIBLICAL PATH OF LIFE 144 LESSON 6

Moses descended the mountain with the two tables of the testimony in hand, which God had written with His own hand. When Joshua heard the noise in the camp, he thought war had broken out, but it was the noise of singing. When Moses came near enough to see the calf and the dancing, he "waxed hot" (which means *to burn, be kindled, be angry, be incensed*). He threw down the tables and broke them. He then took the calf, burned it in the fire, ground it to powder, mixed it with water, and made the people drink it. Aaron then lied about everything. The people had gotten out of control and were not doing what they knew they were to do. Moses demanded a decision. All who were on God's side were to stand with Moses. Anyone who did not stand with Moses was killed—about three thousand men (Exodus 32:25–28). Remember that the people knew what God expected of them, and they had agreed to do it. Because they had not done what they'd promised, there would be a punishment. The next day, Moses told the people how great a sin it was. He then went back up the mount to intercede on the people's behalf. God once again promised that "Angel" would go before them, but God would punish their sin. The Lord plagued the people because of the calf Aaron had made (Exodus 32:30–35).

Moses throws the Tablet of Stone.

LESSON 6　145　THE BIBLICAL PATH OF LIFE

5. They are reminded of the promise, and God with His people

(Exodus 33 and 40)

Even when the people forsook God, He reaffirmed His promise with Moses.

1. And the LORD said unto Moses, Depart, *and* go up hence, thou and the people which thou hast brought up out of the land of Egypt, unto the land which I sware unto Abraham, to Isaac, and to Jacob, saying, Unto thy seed will I give it: 2. And I will send an angel before thee; and I will drive out the Canaanite, the Amorite, and the Hittite, and the Perizzite, the Hivite, and the Jebusite: 3. Unto a land flowing

A cloud covered the tent of the congregation.

with milk and honey: for I will not go up in the midst of thee; for thou art a stiffnecked people: lest I consume thee in the way. (Exodus 33:1–3)

His Angel, Jesus would be with them and go before them.

By Exodus 40 the tabernacle is ready to be set up. They did so and placed all of the implements in their correct places. The glory of the Lord filled the tabernacle. "Then a cloud covered the tent of the congregation, and the glory of the LORD filled the tabernacle" (Exodus 40:34). Moses could not even enter because the cloud was there. The cloud (by day) and the fire (by night) always remained upon the tabernacle for all of the Israelites to see. When it lifted and moved, the people were to follow.

35. And Moses was not able to enter into the tent of the congregation, because the cloud abode thereon, and the glory of the LORD filled the tabernacle. 36. And when the cloud was taken up from over the tabernacle, the children of Israel went onward in all their journeys: 37. But if the cloud were not taken up, then they journeyed not till the day that it was taken up. 38. For the cloud of the LORD *was* upon the tabernacle by day, and fire was on it by night, in the sight of all the house of Israel, throughout all their journeys. (Exodus 40:35–38)

Reinforcement:

Reinforce what you learned in the Bible lesson by again going over the implements of the tabernacle and remembering each piece in its correct places. Remember that each piece is to remind us of Jesus (refer to the part of the lesson, under section 3, that lists the implements of the tabernacle). How is each implement a picture of Christ? We must recognize Jesus.

Also remember that we are the temple of God, and Jesus lives in our hearts. We need to live as if we have Jesus there. Encourage everyone to participate.

Closing:

It would be good to close with a short prayer reinforcing today's lesson. Always include any prayer requests you may have.

Today, pray for God to help us obey His laws and never forsake Him or put other things before Him. Help us to recognize we are a "peculiar treasure" to God.

LESSON 6

Exodus 19–40
God Revealed

Read Exodus 19–40. Complete the following.

1. From where did God speak to Moses? (Exodus 19:2–3) _____
_____

God had delivered them from the Egyptians.

2. What two things did God want them to do? (Exodus 19:5) _____ and _____ Then they would be _____ Then what did God say they would be? (Exodus 19:6) _____ and _____

__A kingdom of priests__ gave them immediate access to God. A relationship was to be established. By having a relationship with God, they placed themselves under His authority to obey Him and His Word.
To become __a holy nation__ required a change in lifestyle; they had to obey God's commands.

3. What was the people's response to God? (Exodus 19:8) _____
_____

LESSON 6   149   THE BIBLICAL PATH OF LIFE

4. When God called the people to the mountain, what did the people see and hear? (Exodus 19:16–19) _____
_____

5. What would happen to the people if they went on the mount? (Exodus 19:12, 21) _____

6. What did God give to the people? (Exodus 20:1–17) _____
_____

7. What do the first four commandments deal with? _____
_____

8. What do the next six commandments deal with? _____
_____

9. What did the people do? (Exodus 20:18–19) _____
_____

10. Why did God want the people to fear him? (Exodus 20:20) __
_____

11. Who did God say He would send before them? (Exodus 23:20) _____ Who was that angel? (Compare Exodus 23:21b to John 10:38b, where Jesus is speaking.) _____
_____
_____

THE BIBLICAL PATH OF LIFE 150 LESSON 6

12. What did the people see when Moses went back up on the mount? (Exodus 24:15–18) _____

_____ How long was he gone? (Exodus 24:18)

_____

13. Why is knowing about the tabernacle important for us today? (2 Corinthians 6:16b) _____

_____

14. What happened in Exodus 32:1–14? _____

_____

15. What did Moses do when he saw the calf? (Exodus 32:19) _____

_____

16. Who had written the two tables of testimony? (Exodus 32:15–16) _____

_____

17. What was upon the tabernacle by day? (Exodus 40:38)_____

_____ By night? _____

Answers:

1. from the mountain in the desert of Sinai; **2.** obey God's voice and keep his covenant; a peculiar treasure; a kingdom of priests and an holy nation; **3.** all God had spoken they would do; **4.** thunder, lightning, and a thick cloud, and heard the voice of a trumpet exceeding loud; **5.** they would die; **6.** the Ten Commandments; **7.** man's relationship with God; **8.** man's relationship with other people; **9.** said for Moses speak to them, they would hear but not God lest they die; **10.** that they sin not; **11.** an angel; Jesus; **12.** a cloud and a devouring fire; forty days and forty nights; **13.** we are the temple of the living God and should remember God is with us; **14.** Aaron took their gold, fashioned a golden calf, and said these be your gods that brought you up out of the land of Egypt; the people offered an offering, worshiped it. God wanted to destroy them, but Moses interceded; **15.** got angry and broke the tables God had written; **16.** God; **17.** cloud; fire)

LESSON 6 **151** THE BIBLICAL PATH OF LIFE

LEVITICUS 1–20
THE WAY TO GOD

LESSON 7

Key Verse

And he [Jesus] is the propitiation for our sins: and not for ours only, but also for the sins of the whole world.

—1 JOHN 2:2

Key Verse Thought: Read today's key verse. *Propitiation* means "the means of putting away sin and establishing righteousness not by man's ability to appease God with any of his offerings, (for man is unable to offer anything to placate God), Jesus is presented as the righteous One; …reconciling us to God, allowing us to be acceptable for fellowship with God (see also Romans 3:25). The propitiation of Christ is very personal—the propitiation for our sins."

By Jesus' death, He cleansed us from sin rather than covering it for a time, as in the Old Testament sacrificial system. God provided His Son as the righteous One (1 John 2:1). So Jesus is the propitiation, made for the whole world (all who would believe), which supplies the method of deliverance from our sin, reconciling us to God and making us acceptable for fellowship with God. We each need to know that we are all sinners, and God cannot look on sin. Only

Jesus can take that sin away (that propitiation). Today's lesson will help us understand the Old Testament sacrificial system. Then we can better understand the sacrifice of Jesus.

Emphasis: Understand that the book of Leviticus shows us the importance of the blood sacrifice needed before we can be reconciled to God, enabling us to have a relationship with Him. Leviticus helps us understand why Jesus, in the New Testament, had to give His life as the one-time-only perfect sacrifice.

Lesson Summary: Once the tabernacle was completed, God spoke to Moses from the tabernacle instead of Mount Sinai. Now that they were free from the land of bondage, the people needed to know how to live as a sanctified people. God instituted the offerings (Leviticus 1–7), the priesthood (Leviticus 8–10; 12–22), and a clean lifestyle for all of His people (Leviticus 11–20). They must understand the foundation of a relationship with God on the basis of the propitiation (appeasement from God's wrath) by a blood sacrifice. Leviticus shows the ability to have fellowship with God when we come to Him as a sanctified people because He is a holy God, and we are a sinful people. Through these many things, the people were to learn how to live as a people wholly given to God in every aspect of their lives.

In the book of Leviticus, "sweet savour" is mentioned sixteen times in reference to the offerings God requires of them. Compare this to what God says in Ephesians 5:2—"And walk in love, as Christ also hath loved us, and hath given himself for us an offering and a sacrifice to God for a sweetsmelling savour." Notice that Jesus' death was a "sweetsmelling savour" to God, once and for all.

LESSON 7 **153** THE BIBLICAL PATH OF LIFE

Suggested Bible Reading to Prepare for This Lesson

- Monday: **Leviticus 1–4**
- Tuesday: **Leviticus 5–8**
- Wednesday: **Leviticus 9–11**
- Thursday: **Leviticus 12–14**
- Friday: **Leviticus 15–17**
- Saturday: **Leviticus 18–20**

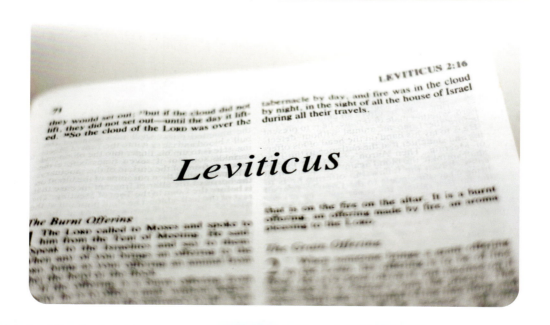

THE BIBLICAL PATH OF LIFE 154 LESSON 7

Leviticus 1–20:
The Way to God

1 The Offerings (Leviticus 1–7)

- God speaks to Moses from the tabernacle and tells him of the different offerings
- The consequences of sins and trespasses
- Instructions to priests; the laws of the offerings (Leviticus 6–7)

2 Priests Chosen and Consecrated (Leviticus 8–10)

- Levites are priests, and they are consecrated, or set apart (Leviticus 8)
- The priests begin to serve (Leviticus 9)
- The strange fire (Leviticus 10:8–11)

3 God's People Are to Be a Clean People (Leviticus 11–20)

- The people are to be personally clean (Leviticus 11–15)
- The Day of Atonement—the nation is to be clean before God (Leviticus 16–17)
- Live a clean lifestyle (Leviticus 18–20)

LESSON 7 **155** THE BIBLICAL PATH OF LIFE

NOTE

Understand the following:

God has revealed himself gradually through the years (remember that Hebrews 1:1 refers to the incremental and progressive manner in which God disclosed Himself up until the appearance of the Son. It was fragmentary and piece by piece, sort of like pieces of a puzzle). We see him as the God of creation in Genesis 1. We then see he is a God who cannot look upon sinful man in Genesis 3. We see that there is a limit to his tolerance of sinful man in Genesis 6 (the flood that destroys the world), yet we also see that God shows grace to those who continually seek him (Noah; Genesis 6:8). God then revealed himself to an individual man (Abraham; Genesis 12) and extended that revelation to his descendants (Exodus 3:15). God showed Himself mightily to His people in the ten plagues and the exodus of His people from bondage (Exodus 7–14). He then showed Himself as their provider (in the wilderness; Exodus 15–17). We see He is a God who expects His people to hear His voice and obey Him (Exodus 19–20). Once the people accomplish the great task of building a tabernacle where God's presence can dwell among His people (Exodus 40), He then reveals just what it takes to become a "clean and forgiven" people in the presence of a sinless, perfect God (Leviticus).

God has mandated a blood sacrifice for man's sins since the garden. When man sinned, God shed the blood of an animal to make a covering for man (for he was naked before God; his sins were exposed). When God

made the clothes to "cover" Adam and Eve, it was a great picture of what the Old Testament sacrifices did for man. They covered mankind's sins for a season. Throughout the Old Testament, we see the shedding of blood (from an animal) to cover mankind's sins. It isn't until we come to Leviticus that God reveals the intricacies and details of the way it is required. The ritualistic sacrifices (explained in Leviticus) that must be fulfilled, completely and perfectly, are to show us the great sacrifice it would take to cleanse sinful man from his sins. It is to reveal to mankind the impossibility of entering into God's presence without the *perfect* sacrifice, only found in Jesus. All throughout the books of the Law we see God gradually reveal Himself to mankind, only a piece at a time, through revelation—only as much as we could handle.

1. The Offerings
(Leviticus 1–7)

Now that they have the tabernacle, they need to understand the sacrifices that are to take place within. We have learned the sacrifices are essential for the covering of sins. What the people had not learned yet is the *why* behind the requirement. That is what the book of Leviticus is for.

God began to speak to Moses from the tabernacle instead of up on the mount. God told him about the different offerings:

- **Chapter 1:** burnt offerings
- **Chapter 2:** meat (or meal) offerings
- **Chapter 3:** peace offerings
- **Chapter 4:** sin offerings
- **Chapter 5 and 7:** trespass offerings
- **Chapter 6:14–23:** grain offerings
- **Chapter 6:24–30:** sin offerings (priests' instructions)
- **Chapter 7:** peace offerings

Notice the consequences of the sin and trespass offerings. "5. And it shall be, when he shall be guilty in one of these *things*, that he shall confess that he hath sinned in that *thing*: 6. And he shall bring his trespass offering unto the LORD for his sin which he hath sinned, a female from the flock, a lamb or a kid of the goats, for a sin offering; and the priest shall make an atonement for him concerning his sin" (Leviticus 5:5–6). The people learned quickly that when they sinned, there was a consequence. They were to bring a lamb or two young turtledoves to kill. The priest would offer the blood of that animal to cover their sins. "And the priest shall make an atonement for him as touching his sin that he hath sinned in one of these, and it shall be forgiven him …" (Leviticus 5:13a). They were to understand that sin was costly.

"For *it is* not possible that the blood of bulls and of goats should take away sins" (Hebrews 10:4). We are reminded that the blood from animals *cannot take* away sin. See what we learn in Hebrews 10:10, 14, "10. By the which will we are sanctified through the offering of the body of Jesus Christ once *for all* … 14. For by one offering he hath perfected for ever them that are sanctified."

God's Tabernacle in the desert.

Jesus offered His body once, the perfect offering, and He had "perfected forever them that are sanctified" (to render clean in a moral sense, to purify). The Israelites looked forward to Jesus' coming and dying on the cross. We look back to the fact that He died on the cross for the sins of mankind. Notice that for both, it takes faith.

God gave the priests specific instructions (Leviticus 6–8).

LESSON 7   159   THE BIBLICAL PATH OF LIFE

2. Priests Chosen and Consecrated
(Leviticus 8–10)

Leviticus 8 showed us the priests had to be set apart and "consecrated" to serve Him. They were to be the mediation between God and man. The Israelites needed to see that they could not approach God because of their sin. Jesus is now our mediator. "For *there is* one God, and one mediator between God and men, the man Christ Jesus" (1 Timothy 2:5).

The priests begin to serve in Leviticus 9. We see Aaron, with the help of his sons, representing the people by offering the sacrifices God required. We understand God was honored through this because of His response, as follows:

> 22. And Aaron lifted up his hand toward the people, and blessed them, and came down from offering of the sin offering, and the burnt offering, and peace offerings. 23. And Moses and Aaron went into the tabernacle of the congregation, and came out, and blessed the people: and the glory of the LORD appeared unto all the people. 24. And there came a fire out from before the LORD, and consumed upon the altar the burnt offering and the fat: *which* when all the people saw, they shouted, and fell on their faces. (Leviticus 9:22–24)

God showed his approval.

Leviticus 10 opens with Aaron's sons offering strange fire, which God had previously commanded them not to offer (Exodus 30:9). Because they disobeyed God, we see they were devoured and died before the Lord.

THE BIBLICAL PATH OF LIFE 160 LESSON 7

3. God's People Are to Be a Clean People
(Leviticus 11–20)

God wanted His people to be clean. Today we understand why it is important. Healthy foods help us to live longer and healthier lives. We also know that germs from unclean things cause sickness and disease. In biblical times, they didn't have this information; they just were to trust God.

- **Chapter 11**—clean and unclean meats
- **Chapter 12–13:46**—bodies are to be clean
- **Chapter 13:47–14:32**—leprosy and clean clothes
- **Chapter 14:33–57**—clean houses
- **Chapter 15**—things you contact are to be clean
- **Chapter 16–17**—Day of Atonement

Day of Atonement.

We see the Day of Atonement (*atonement* in Leviticus 16–17 means "to cover") as the culmination of the cleanliness of the people. Not only are they to be outwardly clean but inwardly as well. One day a year was set apart for the people to put away their sin. It would be covered by the blood sprinkled on the mercy seat. This was a picture for the Israelites (and us today) of what Jesus would one day do for them (and us).

LESSON 7 161 THE BIBLICAL PATH OF LIFE

Finally, we see that we are to be clean in our lifestyles with the rest of humanity. It begins with not looking upon the nakedness of anyone, beginning with family members (Leviticus 18:6–19). It proceeds to tell people to be morally pure with man and beast (Leviticus 18:20–19:37). Emphasize these purities.

The penalties for immorality are listed in Leviticus 20. A couple of verses you may want to specifically notice: "For every one that curseth his father or his mother shall be surely put to death: he hath cursed his father or his mother; his blood *shall be* upon him" (Leviticus 20:9), and "A man also or woman that hath a familiar spirit, or that is a wizard, shall surely be put to death: they shall stone them with stones: their blood *shall be* upon them" (Leviticus 20:27). The latter verse should be emphasized, especially because of the recent popularity of books and movies based on wizards. Christians are to avoid such things. Read Leviticus 20 to see if there are others of which you may want to take note.

The people were supposed to maintain a life that was pleasing to God.

NOTE

Especially notice Leviticus 18:6–19. All of these verses deal with not uncovering or looking upon someone's nakedness. These verses proceed to infidelity (Leviticus 18:20), abortion (Leviticus 18:21), homosexuality (Leviticus 18:22), bestiality (Leviticus 18:23), and the consequences from God, such as disease (Leviticus 18:24–30). Understand that all of these sins begin with looking upon nakedness. People should learn to turn their eyes from any form of nakedness (even partial). Think of commercials, magazine pictures, newspaper ads, movies, the Internet, and so forth.

Reinforcement:

Read the following: "6. Now when these things were thus ordained, the priests went always into the first tabernacle, accomplishing the service *of God*. 7. But into the second *went* the high priest alone once every year, not without blood, which he offered for himself, and *for* the errors of the people" (Hebrews 9:6–7).

9. Which *was* a figure for the time then present, in which were offered both gifts and sacrifices, that could not make him that did the service perfect, as pertaining to the conscience; 10. *Which stood* only in meats and drinks, and divers washings, and carnal ordinances, imposed *on them* until the time of reformation. 11. But Christ being come an high priest of good things to come, by a greater and more perfect tabernacle, not made with hands, that is to say, not of this building; 12. Neither by the blood of goats and calves, but by his own blood he entered in once into the holy place, having obtained eternal redemption *for us*. 13. For if the blood of bulls and of goats, and the ashes of an heifer sprinkling the unclean, sanctifieth to the purifying of the flesh: 14. How much more shall the blood of Christ, who through the eternal Spirit offered himself without spot to God, purge your conscience from dead works to serve the living God? 15. And for

this cause he is the mediator of the new testament, that by means of death, for the redemption of the transgressions *that were* under the first testament, they which are called might receive the promise of eternal inheritance. (Hebrews 9:9–15)

Hebrews 9:6–7 refers to the Day of Atonement (Leviticus 16–17). Hebrews 9:9 begins to reveal to us that this was just a figure, something to help us see physically so we could understand spiritually. It continues to reveal that the blood of Christ, which was offered without spot, is the mediator (the go-between for God and man), and by His death purchased the promise of eternal inheritance for us.

NOTE

Realize just how real sin is, especially in our own lives. If there is sin in our lives, it must be acknowledged. If there is impurity, it must be removed. If there are spiritual defects, they must be purged, not to earn holiness but because we belong to God and seek to obey Him. Think of an area you need to recognize as sin in your life, anything that is not pleasing God. Begin to commit to working on living a clean life before God. A lot of times the sin on the inside shows up on the outside (how you dress, hairstyles, makeup, language, etc.). Remember that God knows each person's heart, and it is that person's job to keep Jesus first there.

THE BIBLICAL PATH OF LIFE   LESSON 7

Closing:

It would be good to close with a short prayer reinforcing today's lesson. Always include any prayer requests you may have. *Today, pray for God to help us to recognize the great sacrifice He made to allow His Son, Jesus, to give His life for us so we would not have to suffer the wrath of God. Pray for help to live a life pleasing to God.*

LESSON 7

Leviticus 1–20
The Way to God

Read Leviticus 1–20. Complete the following.

1. When man sinned in the garden, what did God do? (Genesis 3:21)
_____
_____

   Note: *From Genesis 3, we see that God mandated a blood sacrifice for sin. When man sinned, God shed the blood of an animal to make a covering for man (for he was naked before God; his sins were exposed). When God made the clothes to "cover" Adam and Eve, it was a great picture of what the Old Testament sacrifices did for man. They covered mankind's sins for a season. Throughout the Old Testament we see the shedding of blood (from an animal) to cover mankind's sins. It isn't until we come to Leviticus that God reveals the details of the way it is required. It is to reveal to mankind the impossibility of entering into God's presence without the "perfect" sacrifice, only found in Jesus.*

2. From where does God speak to Moses in Leviticus 1:1? _____
_____

3. What is the first thing one must do when one is guilty of sin? (Leviticus 5:5) _____
_____

THE BIBLICAL PATH OF LIFE 166 LESSON 7

4. In Leviticus 5:6, 9, what was the next step? _____

_____

5. What do we learn in Hebrews 10:4? _____

_____

6. Then what do we learn in Hebrews 10:10, 14? _____

_____

In the Old Testament, they were looking forward to Jesus' death.
Now we look back; both take faith.

7. God chose and set apart the Levites, consecrating them to serve the Lord in the tabernacle. They were the mediator, or go-between, for man and God. Who is our mediator now? (1 Timothy 2:5) _____

8. The priests begin their ministry (Leviticus 9). What was God's response? (Leviticus 9:22–24) _____

_____

Read Leviticus 10:1–2 and Exodus 30:9.

9. What did Nadab and Abihu (Aaron's sons) do wrong? _____

_____

Note: *In the Old Testament, they were looking forward to Jesus' death.*
Now we look back; both take faith.

10. Leviticus 11–15 deals with God's people being clean—their foods, clean bodies, dealing with leprosy (not touching), and having clean houses, and things they came into contact with were to be clean. What do we know today about the importance of cleanliness? _____

_____

11. What was to take place once a year? (Leviticus 16:34) _____

_____

What made the *atonement?* (Leviticus 17:11) _____

_____

12. Read Hebrews 9:11–12. Where did the blood for the redemption of man come from? _____

Atonement means "to cover."
Redemption means "freeing or releasing from guilt and punishment from sin."

13. Does that tell us that we can be forgiven for our sins once and for all? _____

14. Today there are many popular books and movies that have a wizard (or a sorcerer, a magician, a fortune teller, or even a witch; in this verse, wizard can mean any of these) as a hero. What does God say in Leviticus 20:27 to do with these? _____

_____

What should our response be to that? _____

THE BIBLICAL PATH OF LIFE 168 LESSON 7

Answers:

1. God shed the blood of an animal to make a covering for man

2. From the tabernacle

3. Confess that sin

4. Bring a trespass offering to the Lord and sprinkle the blood on the altar

5. It is not possible that the blood of bulls and goats should take away sin

6. Jesus offered His body once, the perfect offering, which sanctifies those who believe, forever

7. Jesus

8. The glory of the Lord appeared and fire came from the Lord and consumed the offering

9. Offered strange fire before the Lord that He had commanded them not to do

10. Healthy foods help us to live longer and healthier lives, and germs from unclean things cause sickness and disease

11. The priest was to make an atonement for the people's sins; the blood

12. Jesus

13. Yes

14. "A man also or woman that hath a familiar spirit, or that is a wizard, shall surely be put to death: they shall stone them with stones: their blood *shall be upon them*"; if God thinks they are worthy of death, we should avoid them)

LEVITICUS 21–27
THE WORSHIP OF GOD

LESSON 8

Key Verse

I am crucified with Christ: nevertheless I live; yet not I, but Christ liveth in me: and the life which I now live in the flesh I live by the faith of the Son of God, who loved me, and gave himself for me.

—GALATIANS 2:20

Key Verse Thought: Read the key verse, making sure you understand it with the following: "I am crucified with Christ *[spiritually by mortifying (putting to death) our worldly and fleshly lusts by the cross of Christ]* …" Now that we have Jesus in our hearts, we can no longer live as we once did (as we want). We live for Jesus because we are given *life* by faith in "the Son of God who loved me, and gave himself for me." Notice the "me" makes it a very personal thing. We especially need to learn to put our "wants" in check. We are not supposed to live our lives doing what we want if we belong to Jesus. We are supposed to allow Him to do what *He* wants to do in our lives!

THE BIBLICAL PATH OF LIFE 170 LESSON 8

Emphasis: To worship God properly, we need to understand that we cannot do what we want to do. We must do what God wants. We are "kings and priests" to God. We have to live our lives "set apart" and pleasing to God so we can offer our lives as a "living sacrifice" (living implies continual, never ending).

Lesson Summary: Once we understand the foundation of fellowship with God (our last lesson), we need to understand the condition in which we must live in order to have a relationship with God and fellowship with Him. God starts with the condition of the priests and then moves on to the condition of their offerings. We find out today (in the New Testament) that when we belong to Jesus, we are "kings and priests" to Him. Knowing this, we need to look at what God required of His priests. They must live a life "set apart." They were to be "holy" before God. This is required of us. We must do as today's key verse tells us—put our worldly lusts to death and live a life pleasing to God.

The book of Leviticus ends with the blessings of obedience, the penalties for disobedience, and the importance of keeping vows to God. A warning is given to always keep our promises to God. (Only about a month's time passes during the book of Leviticus.)

Suggested Bible Reading to Prepare for This Lesson

- Monday: **Leviticus 21**
- Tuesday: **Leviticus 22**
- Wednesday: **Leviticus 23**
- Thursday: **Leviticus 24**
- Friday: **Leviticus 25**
- Saturday: **Leviticus 26–27**

Leviticus 21–27:
The Worship of God

1 **Holiness of the Priests:
Then and Now (Leviticus 21)**

- God-chosen priests are to be holy (Leviticus 21:6)
- We are kings and priests before God because of Jesus (Revelation 1:5–6)
- We are to live clean and holy lives before God (Romans 12:1–2)

2 **The Offerings (Leviticus 22:17–33)**

- Unacceptable offerings (Leviticus 22:17–25)
- Acceptable offerings (Leviticus 22:26–31)
- Our offering today (Romans 12:1–2)

3 **Punishment for Blasphemy or Cursing God
(Leviticus 24)**

- Someone who blasphemed God (Leviticus 24:10–11)
- What God said to do to a blasphemer (Leviticus 24:12–16)
- What Jesus said about a blasphemer (Matthew 12:31–32)

4. Obedience and Disobedience; Tithes (Leviticus 26; 27:26–34)

- Blessings of obedience (Leviticus 26:1–13)
- Penalties for disobedience (Leviticus 26:14–46)
- Tithes (Leviticus 27:26–34)

LESSON 8   173   THE BIBLICAL PATH OF LIFE

1. Holiness of the Priests: Then and Now

(Leviticus 21 and Revelation 1:5–6)

The priests shall be holy unto their God.

God's people were to be set apart from the nations around them as a "peculiar treasure" unto God (as we have already learned in Exodus 19:5). He considered them His possession because He chose them, and He was their provider. Among His people was a group God had set apart for a special purpose. He had chosen them to be the ones who took care of the things of God (including the tabernacle and its implements) and *acted* as the mediator between a holy God and a sinful people (Leviticus 8). God wanted the priests to understand they must take their job very seriously. They must protect the office with utmost care. We already learned they were to be consecrated (set

THE BIBLICAL PATH OF LIFE 174 LESSON 8

apart for a special purpose), but in Leviticus 21, we learn more. "They shall be holy unto their God, and not profane [to desecrate something that is holy] the name of their God: for the offerings of the LORD made by fire, and the bread of their God, they do offer: therefore they shall be holy [apartness, holiness, sacredness]" (Leviticus 21:6). (The words in brackets are added for understanding.) They had a very important job that they had to take very seriously.

Today, because of the sacrifice Jesus made on the cross, we are "kings and priests" unto God. "5. And from Jesus Christ, *who is* the faithful witness, *and* the first begotten of the dead, and the prince of the kings of the earth. Unto him that loved us, and washed us from our sins in his own blood, 6. And hath made us kings [who will one day rule the nations with the Messiah] and priests [Christians are privileged to have access to God offering Him spiritual sacrifices] unto God and his Father; to him be glory and dominion for ever and ever. Amen" (Revelation 1:5–6). (The words in brackets are added for understanding.)

They had a very important job that they had to take very seriously.

NOTE To know how to live a life pleasing to God, read Ephesians 4:17–32.

LESSON 8   175   THE BIBLICAL PATH OF LIFE

2. The Offerings
(Leviticus 22:17–33)

The first part of Leviticus 22 tells us the condition that the priests themselves must be in to serve God. (Review briefly.) It then moves on to the condition of the offering (Leviticus 22:17–25). God first wanted to be sure the priests' hearts and lives were in the right condition to be able to deliver the offerings. That was important. Next, the offering itself had to be right—an offering without spot or blemish—or they were unacceptable (Leviticus 22:19–25). It had to be an offering brought to God in the manner God commanded—no other way. "Therefore shall ye keep my commandments, and do them: I am the LORD" (Leviticus 22:31).

Later, we will see the people have forgotten this. What does God think?

6. A son honoureth *his* father, and a servant his master: if then I *be* a father, where *is* mine honour? and if I *be* a master, where *is* my fear? saith the LORD of hosts unto you, O priests, that despise my name. And ye say, Wherein have we despised thy name? 7. Ye offer polluted bread upon mine altar; and ye say, Wherein have we polluted thee? In that ye say, The table of the LORD *is* contemptible. 8. And if ye offer the blind for sacrifice, *is it* not evil? and if ye offer the lame and sick, *is it* not evil? offer it now unto thy governor; will he be pleased with thee, or accept thy person? saith the LORD of hosts. (Malachi 1:6–8)

THE BIBLICAL PATH OF LIFE 176 LESSON 8

Remember, when we become Christians, Jesus makes us priests (privileged to have access to God, offering Him spiritual sacrifices—praise, our physical bodies, offerings, faith, righteous acts, and more). That tells us that we should live our lives with the same holiness (apart from the world and its ways) as the priests were supposed to do in Leviticus. "I beseech you therefore, brethren, by the mercies of God, that ye present your bodies a living sacrifice, holy, acceptable unto God, which is your reasonable service" (Romans 12:1). Notice that our bodies (the whole person, inside and out) are to be lived as living sacrifices. Everything we do should please God. It then goes on to say, "And be not conformed to this world: but be ye transformed by the renewing of your mind, that ye may prove what is that good, and acceptable, and perfect, will of God" (Romans 12:2). Christians have to live lives totally different from the way the world lives. We should be very careful to live our lives clean and holy before God.

The priests themselves must be right in order to serve God.

LESSON 8　177　THE BIBLICAL PATH OF LIFE

3. Punishment for Blasphemy or Cursing God
(Leviticus 24)

There was a son of an Israelite woman who strove with another Israelite. He blasphemed the name of the Lord and cursed it. "And the Israelitish woman's son blasphemed the name *of the LORD*, and cursed. And they brought him unto Moses: (and his mother's name *was* Shelomith, the daughter of Dibri, of the tribe of Dan)" (Leviticus 24:11). *Blasphemed* means "to speak profanely (showing disregard or contempt) of God, or to God; to curse or revile; to show contempt for God or the things of God." They locked him up while God showed them what to do. God said for everyone who heard him blaspheme to lay their hands on him. Then the people were to stone him. The same would happen to anyone who cursed God. "15. And thou shalt speak unto the children of Israel, saying, Whosoever curseth his God shall bear his sin. 16. And he that blasphemeth the name of the LORD, he shall surely be put to death, *and* all the congregation shall certainly stone him: as well the stranger, as he that is born in the land, when he blasphemeth the name *of the LORD*, shall be put to death" (Leviticus 24:15–16).

But that was in the Old Testament. In the New Testament, we see what Jesus said about cursing.

Because Jesus died on the cross, any sin can be forgiven—all but one. "31. Wherefore I say unto you, All manner of sin and blasphemy shall be forgiven unto men: but the blasphemy *against the Holy* Ghost shall not be forgiven unto men. 32. And whosoever speaketh a word against the Son of man, it shall be forgiven him: but whosoever speaketh against the Holy Ghost, it shall not be forgiven him, neither in this world, neither in the *world* to come" (Matthew 12:31–32). To understand this better, we need to see what happened just before Jesus said these words. The Pharisees had challenged Jesus' authority. Jesus knew the Pharisees' thoughts. Jesus recognized they rejected Him *and* the authority God had given Him (displayed by the Holy Ghost).

Does that mean it is hopeless if you blasphemed before you knew it was wrong?

We see a great example of this in Paul. "Who was before a blasphemer, and a persecutor, and injurious: but I obtained mercy, because I did *it* ignorantly in unbelief" (1 Timothy 1:13). Paul not only became a Christian but a mighty missionary, spreading the Gospel message into the world.

Paul spread the Gospel message into the world.

LESSON 8 179 THE BIBLICAL PATH OF LIFE

4. Obedience and Disobedience; Tithes
(Leviticus 26; 27:26–34)

God promised to bless His people if they would obey His commands (read Leviticus 26:1–13). He also reaffirmed that promise God had made to their forefathers. "For I will have respect unto you, and make you fruitful, and multiply you, and establish my covenant with you" (Leviticus 26:9). Notice He added something more. "12. And I will walk among you, and will be your God, and ye shall be my people. 13. I *am* the LORD your God, which brought you forth out of the land of Egypt, that ye should

> The sting of death is sin; and the strength of sin is the law.

THE BIBLICAL PATH OF LIFE — 180 — LESSON 8

not be their bondmen; and I have broken the bands of your yoke, and made you go upright" (Leviticus 26:12–13).

When Jesus died for mankind's sins and then rose again, He "broke the bands of your yoke" (Leviticus 26:13). Remember Romans 6:23—"The wages of sin is death …"—but look at 1 Corinthians 15:55–57, which tells us, "55. O death, where *is* thy sting? O grave, where *is* thy victory? 56. The sting of death *is* sin; and the strength of sin is the law. 57. But thanks *be* to God, which giveth us the victory through our Lord Jesus Christ."

Jesus gives Christians the victory over the "sting of death." *But notice* that if they disobeyed God's commands, He would curse His people (read Leviticus 26:14–46). Most of Leviticus 26 is a warning of what would happen to God's people if they did *not* obey His commands. Obedience is *very* important to God.

As Christians, we become the children of Abraham. We receive the blessings promised to him and his descendants. "6. Even as Abraham believed God, and it was accounted to him for righteousness. 7. Know ye therefore that they which are of faith, the same are the children of Abraham. 8. And the scripture, foreseeing that God would justify the heathen through faith, preached before the gospel unto Abraham, *saying,* In thee shall all nations be blessed. 9. So then they which be of faith are blessed with faithful Abraham" (Galatians 3:6–9). Knowing this, we *must* obey God's Word.

The book of Leviticus ends with a confirmation that the people are to give their tithes to God from their "firstfruits." It should be the first thing His people do when they receive something (money or otherwise). "30. And all the tithe of the land, *whether* of the seed of the land, *or* of the fruit of the tree, *is* the LORD'S: *it is* holy unto the LORD. 31. And if a man will at all redeem *ought* of his tithes, he shall add thereto the fifth *part* thereof. 32. And concerning the tithe of the herd, or of the flock, *even* of whatsoever passeth under the rod, the tenth shall be holy unto the LORD" (Leviticus 27:30–32).

LESSON 8 181 THE BIBLICAL PATH OF LIFE

In Conclusion:

Compare today's lesson with 1 John 1:5–7, which says, "5. This then is the message which we have heard of him, and declare unto you, that God is light, and in him is no darkness at all. 6. If we say that we have fellowship with him, and walk in darkness, we lie, and do not the truth: 7. But if we walk in the light, as he is in the light, we have fellowship one with another, and the blood of Jesus Christ his Son cleanseth us from all sin."

Notice that God is perfect and sinless (God is light, and in Him is no darkness), and we cannot have fellowship with Him and live a sinful life (walk in darkness). Because Jesus' blood cleansed those who ask Him (those who become Christians), Christians now walk in the light (live lives pleasing to God) and have fellowship with Him (a relationship.) All of this was pictured in the book of Leviticus.

Leviticus 21 – 27 at a Glance:

- **Leviticus 21:** Holiness of priests
- **Leviticus 22:** Laws concerning priests (1-16), unacceptable offerings (17-25), acceptable offerings (26-33)
- **Leviticus 23:** Feasts
- **Leviticus 24:** Tending the lamps (1-4), 12 loaves – showbread (5-9), punishment for blasphemy (10-16, 23), crimes worthy of death (17-22)
- **Leviticus 25:** Sabbath of land – Year of Jubilee (1-34), redeeming the poor (35-55)

- **Leviticus 26:** Blessings of obedience and penalties for *disobedience*
- **Leviticus 27:** Redemption of vows (1-13), sanctification of house and possessions (14-25), tithes (26-34)

Reinforcement:

Think of ways you can be a "living sacrifice." Remember that Christians are "kings and priests" to God (if one belongs to Him). We should live our lives pleasing to God, knowing that He gave His Son, Jesus, for that honor and privilege. Consider at least one area in your life where you will make a concerted effort to improve.

Closing:

It would be good to close with a short prayer reinforcing today's lesson. Always include any prayer requests you may have. *Today, pray for God to help us put our selfish desires to death and live a life pleasing to God, obeying Him, so He will bless our lives, and we will not see the "curses" of disobedience.*

LESSON 8 183 THE BIBLICAL PATH OF LIFE

LESSON 8

Leviticus 21–27:
The Worship of God

Read Leviticus 21–27. Complete the following.

1. Remember Exodus 19:5–6? What were the people to do? _____
_____ and
_____ Then they would be
_____ Then what did God say they would be?
_____ and
_____

Remember: "A kingdom of priests" gave them immediate access to God. A relationship was to be established. By having a relationship with God, they placed themselves under His authority; to obey Him and His Word. To become "a holy nation" required a change in lifestyle; they had to obey God's commands.

2. God had chosen the tribe of Levi to be the priests and act as the mediator (go-between) for sinful man and God. What were they to be? (Leviticus 21:6b) _____

Holy: "means "to be set apart, perfect, in a moral sense." They were to be pure in heart; free from sin and sinful affections and live a sacred life pleasing to God.

THE BIBLICAL PATH OF LIFE 184 LESSON 8

3. Today, we know something important: when Jesus washed away our sins, He did something special. What was it? (Revelation 1:5b–6) He made us ____ _____ and _____ unto God.

As kings we will one day rule the nations with Jesus.

As priests we have access to God.

4. First, the priests' hearts and lives had to be in the right condition to be able to deliver the offering. What do we see about the offering? (Leviticus 22:18–21) _____

As priests, also living separate lives, we have access to

God to offer Him spiritual sacrifices.

5. According to Romans 12:1, what are we to do? _____ _____

Everything we do with our bodies (inside and out) should please God.

6. What does it tell us to do in Romans 12:2? _____ _____

As Christians, we must live our lives totally

different from the way the world lives.

7. What did the Israelitish woman's son do? (Leviticus 24:11) _____ _____ Why did they lock him up (put him in ward)? (Leviticus 24:12) _____ What were they to do to this son who blasphemed God and cursed? (Leviticus 24:14) _____

Blaspheme: *"to speak of God in terms of impious irreverence;*

to revile or speak reproachfully"

LESSON 8 **185** THE BIBLICAL PATH OF LIFE

8. What was to happen to anyone who did the same thing? (Leviticus 24:15–16) _____

_____

9. Have you ever known anyone who has cursed or even used God's name in vain? _____ Isn't that what this woman's son did? _____ After hearing this, should you be very careful with what you say? _____

That was in the Old Testament.
Read on to see what the New Testament tells us.

10. Jesus died on the cross to forgive us of our sins. According to Matthew 12:31–32, what will be forgiven? _____ _____ What will not be forgiven? _____

11. What does Jesus go on to say in Matthew 12:36? _____ _____

Be very careful what you say. Mathew 12:37 tells us that
by our own words we will be justified or condemned.

12. If they walk with God, what does He promise? (Leviticus 26:9)
_____

And (Leviticus 26:12) _____

_____

THE BIBLICAL PATH OF LIFE **186** LESSON 8

13. Read 1 John 1:5–7. What should we do? _____

Then what will Jesus do? _____

_____

Notice that 1 John 1:5–7 is a picture of what Leviticus is all about.
Walk in the Light!

Answers:

1. Obey God's voice; keep his covenant; a peculiar treasure; a kingdom of priests; an holy nation

2. They shall be holy

3. Kings; priests

4. It must be perfect with no blemish

5. Present ourselves (the whole person, inside and out) as living sacrifices, acceptable unto God

6. Be transformed by the renewing of our mind – knowing God's will for my life; **7.** blasphemed the name of the Lord and cursed; to find out what God would have them do with him; bring him forth and stone him

7. Put him to death

8. Most likely the answer is yes; yes; yes. **9.** Offered strange fire before the Lord that He had commanded them not to do

10. All manner of sin and blasphemy shall be forgiven unto men; blasphemy against the Holy Ghost shall not be forgiven

11. People will give account for every idle word spoken in the day of judgment

12. He will respect them; make them fruitful, multiply them, and establish His covenant with them; walk among them, be their God, and they'll be His people

13. Walk in the light; we will have fellowship one with another, and the blood of Jesus Christ will cleanse us from all sin)

LESSON 8 **187** THE BIBLICAL PATH OF LIFE

NUMBERS 1–19
WANDERING IN THE WILDERNESS

LESSON 9

Key Verse

Take heed, brethren, lest there be in any of you an evil heart of unbelief, in departing from the living God.

—HEBREWS 3:12

Key Verse Thought: Read today's key verse. Understand it with the following: *Take heed* means "to beware, or pay attention to." Christians need to be careful to *not* have an evil heart (any form of evil) that would cause them to quit believing in God or His ways. Today we see where the people depart from the living God. When a Christian chooses his own will over God's, he has departed from God. This verse is a warning.

Emphasis: Today we will see the children of Israel have hearts of unbelief and depart from the plans the living God had for them. We must believe God's Word, or we will spend our lives wandering, just like the children of Israel did in the wilderness.

THE BIBLICAL PATH OF LIFE **188** LESSON 9

Lesson Summary: The name Numbers comes from a numbering of the people at the beginning of the book and then again at the end. These were two different groups of people. This book is another testimony to the orderliness of our God. This week we look at the old generation and the many troubles they caused Moses. When the twelve spies were sent into the land (the land promised to Abraham), only Joshua and Caleb brought back a good report, claiming God would allow them to conquer the land. When the Israelites disobeyed God's command to cross over into the Promised Land, they were disciplined. The old generation would die and not enter into the Promised Land because they refused to obey God's command. Joshua and Caleb were the only ones to escape God's discipline (wandering in the wilderness for forty years and missing the Promised Land).

Within we also find more murmurings of the people and their discipline. Fewer than forty years elapsed during the book of Numbers. Throughout Numbers, we will see God guiding, providing, and protecting His people in spite of their constant hearts of unbelief. God stayed with them, even when they departed from Him and His Word.

Suggested Bible Reading to Prepare for This Lesson

⊘ Monday: **Numbers 1–3**   ⊘ Thursday: **Numbers 10–12**

⊘ Tuesday: **Numbers 4–6**   ⊘ Friday: **Numbers 13–15**

⊘ Wednesday: **Numbers 7–9**   ⊘ Saturday: **Numbers 16–19**

LESSON 9 THE BIBLICAL PATH OF LIFE

Numbers 1–19:
Wandering in the Wilderness

1   God Numbered and Organized His People

- Numbered by tribes (Numbers 1)
- Camp is arranged (Numbers 2)
- Passover observed (Numbers 9)

2   Moses' Troubles with the People

- People complain; fire consumes (Numbers 11:1–3)
- People want meat; plague ensues (Numbers 11:4–35)
- Miriam and Aaron rebel; leprosy on Miriam (Numbers 12)

3   People to Take the Promised Land

- Twelve spies sent; ten say no and two say yes (Numbers 13)
- The people rebel and refuse to enter; Moses intercedes (Numbers 14:1–19)

- God punishes their disobedience—forty years wandering promised (Numbers 14:20–39)
- People reject God's Word and try enter the land (Numbers 14:40–45)

4 More Troubles with the People

- Man breaks Sabbath law; a reminder to obey (Numbers 15:32–41)
- Korah's rebellion (Numbers 16:1–40)
- People murmur against Moses and Aaron (Numbers 16:41–50)

1. God Numbered and Organized His People
(Numbers 1–2; 9)

God is a God of order. The book of Numbers begins with a census. The people are numbered by tribes and organized. The tabernacle is set up in the center of camp (making God's presence as the central focal point). God then gave Moses specific instructions as to the placement of each tribe's camp. There were to be three tribes encamped on each side of the tabernacle. When the placement was complete, it was in the form of a cross (with the tabernacle as the center).

By Numbers 9, after the camp was arranged, we find it was time to keep the Passover. "4. And Moses spake unto the children of Israel, that they should keep the Passover. 5. And they kept the Passover on the fourteenth day of the first month at even in the wilderness of Sinai: according to all that the LORD commanded Moses, so did the children of Israel" (Numbers 9:4–5). They were to remember what God had done for them in their release from bondage in Egypt.

It is interesting that when the tribes were arranged around the tabernacle, they formed the shape of a cross. Emphasize that God wanted them to recognize that everything was to be centered on Him. He wants the same thing from us today. That is why we refer to Jesus as being in our hearts. That is the center of our beings (emotional and physical).

THE BIBLICAL PATH OF LIFE 192 LESSON 9

2. Moses' Troubles with the People
(Numbers 11–12)

"**1.** And *when* the people complained, it displeased the LORD: and the LORD heard it; and his anger was kindled; and the fire of the LORD burnt among them, and consumed *them that were* in the uttermost parts of the camp. 2. And the people cried unto Moses; and when Moses prayed unto the LORD, the fire was quenched" (Numbers 11:1–2).

They did not learn. See how quickly the children of Israel "wept again" (which means *to complain*). "And the mixt multitude that was among them fell a lusting: and the children of Israel also wept again, and said, Who shall give us flesh to eat?" (Numbers 11:4). They were no longer content with the manna God provided for them each morning. Instead, they remember the pleasantries they had in the land of bondage. They didn't remember the bondage or that they had cried out for God to deliver them from that bondage. Read about the versatility of the manna, *"And* the people went about, and gathered *it*, and ground *it* in mills, or beat *it* in a mortar, and baked *it* in pans, and made cakes of it: and the taste of it was as the taste of fresh oil" (Numbers 11:8), yet see that they remained unsatisfied with it. They wanted meat. Moses told God he had had enough. Someone had to help him with these complaining people.

14. I am not able to bear all this people alone, because *it is* too heavy for me. 15. And if thou deal thus with me, kill me, I pray thee, out of hand, if I have found favour

LESSON 9 193 THE BIBLICAL PATH OF LIFE

in thy sight; and let me not see my wretchedness. 16. And the LORD said unto Moses, Gather unto me seventy men of the elders of Israel, whom thou knowest to be the elders of the people, and officers over them; and bring them unto the tabernacle of the congregation, that they may stand there with thee. 17. And I will come down and talk with thee there: and I will take of the spirit which *is* upon thee, and will put *it* upon them; and they shall bear the burden of the people with thee, that thou bear *it* not thyself alone. (Numbers 11:14–17)

God told Moses to gather seventy men. God's Spirit would be on these men, allowing them to help him "bear the burden."

Afterward, God gave the people what they wanted. They would have flesh to eat—until it came out of their noses.

18. And say thou unto the people, Sanctify yourselves against to morrow, and ye shall eat flesh: for ye have wept in the ears of the LORD, saying, Who shall give us flesh to eat? for *it was* well with us in Egypt: therefore the LORD will give you flesh, and ye shall eat. 19. Ye shall not eat one day, nor two days, nor five days, neither ten days, nor twenty days; 20. *But* even a whole month, until it come out at your nostrils, and it be loathsome unto you: because that ye have despised the LORD which *is* among you, and have wept before him, saying, Why came we forth out of Egypt? (Numbers 11:18–20)

He had quail come in from the sea in a wind from the Lord. "And there went forth a wind from the LORD, and brought quails from the sea, and let *them* fall by the camp, as it were a day's journey on this side, and as it were a day's journey on the other side, round about the camp, and as it were two cubits *high* upon the face of the earth" (Numbers 11:31). The people had their meat. While they consumed upon their own lust (ate the meat they so desired or lusted after), God's anger was kindled, and He sent a plague among his people. The people had to bury those who had lusted. "33. And while the flesh *was* yet between their teeth, ere it was chewed, the wrath of the LORD was kindled against the people, and the LORD smote the people with a very great plague. 34.

> Lord brought quails from the sea, and let them fall by the camp.

INTRODUCTION 195 THE BIBLICAL PATH OF LIFE

And he called the name of that place Kibrothhattaavah: because there they buried the people that lusted" (Numbers 11:33–34). They should have been content with what God had given them. Today, we can read a verse in Hebrews to help us remember this. *"Let your* conversation *be* without covetousness; *and be* content with such things as ye have …" (Hebrews 13:5a).

Not only were the people trouble for Moses, but even his own brother and sister caused him grief. Notice the kind of man Moses was: "Now the man Moses was very meek, above all the men which were upon the face of the earth" (Numbers 12:3). In Numbers 12, we see Aaron and Miriam had spoken against Moses. "1. And Miriam and Aaron spake against Moses because of the Ethiopian woman whom he had married: for he had married an Ethiopian woman. 2. And they said, Hath the LORD indeed spoken only by Moses? hath he not spoken also by us? And the LORD heard it" (Numbers 12:1–2). There is something that even Aaron and Miriam hadn't realized. Read the following: "The eyes of the LORD are in every place, beholding the evil and the good" (Proverbs 15:3). God had given Aaron to Moses to help him. Remember Exodus 7:1–2, which says, "1. And the LORD said unto Moses, See, I have made thee a god to Pharaoh:

Aaron and Miriam speaking against Moses.

and Aaron thy brother shall be thy prophet. 2. Thou shalt speak all that I command thee: and Aaron thy brother shall speak unto Pharaoh, that he send the children of Israel out of his land."

Suddenly, that was not good enough. They thought of themselves better than they ought. "For I say, through the grace given unto me, to every man that is among you, not to think *of himself* more highly than he ought to think …" (Romans 12:3a). When we think too highly of ourselves, we prepare ourselves for a fall. "Wherefore let him that thinketh he standeth take heed lest he fall" (1 Corinthians 10:12). We see God struck Miriam with leprosy. "9. And the anger of the LORD was kindled against them; and he departed. 10. And the cloud departed from off the tabernacle; and, behold, Miriam *became* leprous, *white* as snow: and Aaron looked upon Miriam, and, behold, *she was* leprous" (Numbers 12:9–10).

Because of repentance and Moses' prayer, she was healed.

> 11. And Aaron said unto Moses, Alas, my lord, I beseech thee, lay not the sin upon us, wherein we have done foolishly, and wherein we have sinned. 12. Let her not be as one dead, of whom the flesh is half consumed when he cometh out of his mother's womb. 13. And Moses cried unto the LORD, saying, Heal her now, O God, I beseech thee. 14. And the LORD said unto Moses, If her father had but spit in her face, should she not be ashamed seven days? let her be shut out from the camp seven days, and after that let her be received in *again*. 15. And Miriam was shut out from the camp seven days: and the people journeyed not till Miriam was brought in *again*. (Numbers 12:11–15)

3. People to Take the Promised Land
(Numbers 13–14)

> **People decided to enter into the land disobeying God.**

Remember, God was taking them to the Promised Land. Read Numbers 13–14 to refresh your memory of the twelve spies. Ten said they could not take the land; two said they could because God said they could. Because the people decided with the ten, God would not allow them to enter into the land. Every one of that generation would die, except for the two who believed God: Joshua and Caleb. When the people realized they should have done as God told them, they decided to enter the land. In spite of the warning not to go, the people went anyway. Notice that in Numbers 14:44, neither God nor Moses went with them. The people were defeated.

The majority was wrong. Note that God wants us to trust Him. Also note that God honored the only two men who were willing to walk with Him. Out of the millions of people, they were the only two who were allowed to enter the Promised Land.

THE BIBLICAL PATH OF LIFE — 198 — LESSON 9

4. More Troubles with the People
(Numbers 15:32–16:50)

It's important to remember that obedience is extremely important to God. The people in the Old Testament usually had a very hard time remembering this. God often reminded them just how important obedience is to Him. "2. Six days shall work be done, but on the seventh day there shall be to you an holy day, a sabbath of rest to the LORD: whosoever doeth work therein shall be put to death. 3. Ye shall kindle no fire throughout your habitations upon the sabbath day" (Exodus 35:2–3).

Then read the following:

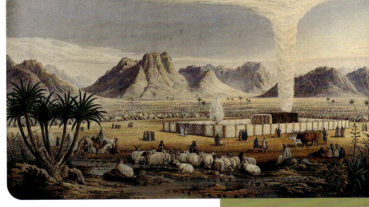

The Israelites' encampment in the wilderness.

32. And while the children of Israel were in the wilderness, they found a man that gathered sticks upon the sabbath day. 33. And they that found him gathering sticks brought him unto Moses and Aaron, and unto all the congregation. 34. And they put him in ward, because it was not declared what should

be done to him. 35. And the LORD said unto Moses, The man shall be surely put to death: all the congregation shall stone him with stones without the camp. 36. And all the congregation brought him without the camp, and stoned him with stones, and he died; as the LORD commanded Moses. (Numbers 15:32–36)

Did you notice the grave example in these verses? Understand that even when you do something that doesn't seem like it will hurt anybody else, and it may even do someone some good, if God said not to do it, you should not do it. God said the Sabbath was a day of rest. They were not to even "kindle a fire" (burn a fire).

Korah led a rebellion of the people against God and Moses. He basically did the same thing that Aaron and Miriam had done in Numbers 12, only Korah brought 250 "princes of the assembly" with him.

Read Numbers 16 to remember what happened when a group of people rose up against God's chosen leader. In Numbers 16:28, Moses reiterated that God was the one who placed him in the place of leadership. God opened up the earth, and it swallowed everyone alive into the pit that stood with Korah, including their houses and their goods. It should be a warning to us, even today, not to reject the man God has placed in a position of authority, even under the guise of "helping" him (see Numbers 16:3—ye take too much upon you).

Even after this mighty display, the people murmured against Moses and Aaron and said that they had killed all of those people. Read Numbers 16:41–50 to see God discipline the people once again for murmuring against what God was doing. Especially notice Moses' constant intercession before God on behalf of the people. When Moses prayed for God to spare the people, God once again stayed His hand and the plague ended.

NOTE Emphasize that just because someone says it is okay to do something, that doesn't necessarily make it so. Obeying God should always be most important! (Remember the man who gathered sticks on the Sabbath in Numbers 15:32-36?)

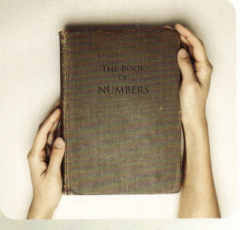

With Korah's rebellion, recognize that Moses was God's man. No one should ever go against God's man. Even if he is wrong (as when Moses struck the rock instead of speaking to it), he is the one accountable to God, and he will be the one disciplined. (Moses was not allowed to enter the Promised Land, but there were no consequences for the people for that act of disobedience.) Remember Hebrews 13:17—"Obey them that have the rule over you, and submit yourselves: for they watch for your souls, as they that must give account, that they may do it with joy, and not with grief: for that *is* unprofitable for you."

Numbers 1-19 at a Glance:

- **Chapter 1:** Number of the people (by tribes)
- **Chapter 2:** How to arrange the camp
- **Chapter 3:** Duties of Levites (1-10), Levites to serve God & they are numbered (11-39)

- **Chapter 4:** Duties divided among the Levites
- **Chapter 5:** Lepers put out of camp (1-4), sin – guilt – recompense (5-10), Law concerning jealousy (11-31)
- **Chapter 6:** Nazarite's vow & their laws (1-21), blessing at the end of the laws (22-27)
- **Chapter 7:** The first official offering, and a listing of the offering, from the head of each tribe
- **Chapter 8:** Lighting of lamps and Levites are again consecrated
- **Chapter 9:** Observance of Passover (1-14), moving of cloud (15-23)
- **Chapter 10:** 2 silver trumpets (1-10), listing of head of tribes (11-28), Hobab leaves (29-32), leave Mt. Sinai (33-36)
- **Chapter 11:** People complain – fire consumes (1-3), complain for meat, 70 elders called, get quail, & punished
- **Chapter 12:** Miriam & Aaron raise up against Moses – Miriam struck with leprosy
- **Chapter 13:** 12 spies set to search Canaan for 40 days – 10 say no, 2 say yes
- **Chapter 14:** People say no, Joshua tries to persuade, 40 years wandering promised, people go without God
- **Chapter 15:** Instructions for entering land (1-31), man gathered sticks on Sabbath (32-36), fringe reminder (37-41)
- **Chapter 16:** Korah's rebellion (1-40), people complain, Moses intercedes, plague stayed (41-50)
- **Chapter 17:** Aaron's rod buds
- **Chapter 18:** Portion for priests
- **Chapter 19:** Red heifer (ashes) and purify for uncleaness

THE BIBLICAL PATH OF LIFE 202 LESSON 9

Reinforcement:

Recognize the importance of following God's will. The people could have entered the land if they had only trusted God and obeyed Him. Remember these events that took place in the book of Numbers and the lessons that should be learned as well, the most important one being not to depart from God and His will for each person's life. Don't forget to apply Hebrews 13:17 to your life, always submitting yourself to your authority (God, employer, pastor, police officer, etc.) and trusting God with the consequences.

Closing:

It would be good to close with a short prayer reinforcing today's lesson. Always include any prayer requests you may have. *Today, pray for God to help us always believe what it says in God's Word. Pray for us to not have hearts of unbelief but to walk with God and never leave Him.*

LESSON 9   THE BIBLICAL PATH OF LIFE

LESSON 9

Numbers 1–19:
Wandering in the Wilderness

Read Numbers 1–19. Complete the following.

1. From where does God speak to Moses, and what was he to do? (Numbers 1:1–2) _____
_____

This is the first numbering of the people (all over age twenty) in the book of Numbers.

2. Where was the tabernacle to be in relation to the encampment? (Numbers 2:17) _____

With the tabernacle in the center and the camps on all four sides, it formed the shape of a cross.

3. Once the people are numbered and organized, it is time to keep what? (Numbers 9:4) _____

4. What did the people do? (Numbers 11:1) _____
What four things happened? _____
_____
_____
_____

THE BIBLICAL PATH OF LIFE   LESSON 1

5. What did Moses do when the people cried? (Numbers 11:2) _____
What did God do? _____

_____

6. What did the people want? (Numbers 11:4) _____ What were they
tired of? (Numbers 11:6) _____ How did Moses feel about the complaining?
(Numbers 11:10, 14) _____ How did
God help Moses? (Numbers 11:16–17) _____

7. Did God give the people what they wanted? (Numbers 11:31) _____ What
was it? _____ What did God do because the people desired and took?
(Numbers 11:33) _____

8. What can we learn from this event? (Hebrews 13:5a) _____

_____

9. Who else gave Moses trouble? (Numbers 12:1–2) _____
_____ Does God know all? (Proverbs 15:3) _____ What happened
to Miriam? (Numbers 12:9–10) _____
Who prayed for Miriam? (Numbers 12:13)_____ Was his prayer
answered? (Numbers 12:15)

10. What did God tell the people to do? (Numbers 13:1–2) _____
_____ How many went? _____ How many days were
they gone? (Numbers 13:25) _____ What did they bring back? (Numbers 13:23)
But what was the report? (Numbers 13:27–28, 31–33) _____
_____ What did Caleb say? (Numbers 13:30) _____

_____

LESSON 1 **205** THE BIBLICAL PATH OF LIFE

11. What did the people say? (Numbers 14:4–9) _____
_____ What did Joshua and Caleb do?
_____

What was the people's response? (Numbers 14:10a) _____
_____

12. Was God pleased with the people's response? (Numbers 14:11)
_____ What did He want to do? (Numbers 14:12) _____
_____ What did Moses pray? (Numbers 14:19)
God's answer? (Numbers 14:20) _____ But what was their punishment? (Numbers 14:23, 35) _____

13. Who led a rebellion? (Numbers 16:1–3) _____
What was Moses' response? (Numbers 16:4–5) _____
_____

Against whom did he really rebel? _____ What happened to all
who stood with Korah? (Numbers 16:29–33) _____
_____
_____

Answers:

1. From the tabernacle and he was to number all of the people

2. Center

3. Passover

4. Complained; it displeased the Lord, anger was kindled, fire burn among them, consumed them

5. Moses prayed; the fire was quenched

6. Flesh (meat); manna; Moses was displeased; God gave Moses seventy men to stand with him, and they would help bear the burden of the people

7. Yes; quail; smote them with a great plague

8. Be content with such things as ye have

9. Miriam and Aaron; yes; she was struck with leprosy; Moses; yes

10. Send a man from each tribe to search out Canaan; twelve; forty days; huge cluster of grapes, pomegranates, figs; the land flows with milk and honey, the cities are walled and great, there were giants; let us go up at once and possess it

11. Make a captain and return to Egypt; told them to not rebel against the Lord, the Lord is with them so fear them not; they wanted to stone Joshua and Caleb

12. No; smite them, disinherit them, make a mighty nation of Moses; pardon this people of their iniquity, forgive them; God pardoned; wouldn't see the land, wander in the wilderness for 40 years and die there; Joshua and Caleb

13. Korah; fell on his face; tomorrow God would show who was His; God; the earth opened up, swallowed them and their houses and goods, and they perished)

NUMBERS 20–36
THE NEXT GENERATION

LESSON 10

Key Verse

Let us hear the conclusion of the whole matter: Fear God, and keep his commandments: for this is the whole duty of man.

—ECCLESIASTES 12:13

Key Verse Thought: Can you name any of God's commandments? Understand that fearing God does not mean being afraid of Him. *Fear* means "morally to revere; a dread of His wrath; and a reverence of His majesty." It is knowing what He expects of us and then doing it.

Today we see what happened to God's people when they did not keep God's commandments. They did not understand what we should understand today: our entire duty *is* to fear God and keep His commands.

Emphasis: The most important thing is to reverence God and keep His commandments. That is the fear of God. It is our duty.

THE BIBLICAL PATH OF LIFE **208** LESSON 10

Lesson Summary: We have been looking at the first generation to leave Egypt. That generation is now dying, and the new generation is developing. This week, we continue with the wandering of the people in the wilderness. We will see Miriam die, look at the fiery serpents and the salvation offered through the serpent lifted up, and look at the life of Balaam. We also will see what happens to a disobedient people. Moses is told he will die, and Joshua will be appointed the new leader. Finally, we will see the new generation numbered and prepared to enter the Promised Land. But that promise to enter comes with a warning.

In Numbers, we see God guiding, providing, protecting, and even disciplining His people until they reach the Promised Land. As they prepare to enter, Joshua is introduced as the successor to Moses (Numbers 27:15–23).

Suggested Bible Reading to Prepare for This Lesson

⊘	Monday:	**Numbers 20–22**
⊘	Tuesday:	**Numbers 23–25**
⊘	Wednesday:	**Numbers 26–28**
⊘	Thursday:	**Numbers 29–31**
⊘	Friday:	**Numbers 32–34**
⊘	Saturday:	**Numbers 35–36**

LESSON 10 **209** THE BIBLICAL PATH OF LIFE

Numbers 20–36:
The Next Generation

1   **A Wandering People (Numbers 20–21)**

- Miriam died (Numbers 20:1)
- No water; Moses spoke and smote (Numbers 20:2–11)
- Moses' and Aaron's punishment (Numbers 20:12–13)
- Fiery serpents (Numbers 21:4–9)

2   **Balaam and His Choice (Numbers 22–24)**

- Balaam's donkey (Numbers 22)
- Balaam's prophecies (Numbers 23)
- Balaam blesses Israel (Numbers 24)
- A promise of Jesus (Numbers 24:17)

3   **A Disobedient People (Numbers 25)**

- What happened when the people worshiped idols (Numbers 25:1–5)
- What happened when one brought in a Midianite woman (Numbers 25:6–9)

THE BIBLICAL PATH OF LIFE **210** LESSON 10

- Phinehas blessed for doing right (Numbers 25:10–18)

4. Final Provisions before Entering the Promised Land (Numbers 26–36)

- New generation numbered & how land is to be divided (Numbers 26:1–56)
- Only Caleb and Joshua live to enter Promised Land (Numbers 26:63–65)
- Moses sees Promised Land; Joshua chosen and charged (Numbers 27:12–23)
- The promise of conquest with a warning (Numbers 33:50–56)

1. A Wandering People
(Numbers 20-21)

Today we see that the people are beginning to see the fulfillment of God's chastisement on them. Miriam died. Remember that everyone twenty years old and older would die in the wilderness because they refused to trust God and enter the Promised Land when God told them to go.

Living in the wilderness, a desert land, they found they once again had no water. Immediately, the people went to Moses and Aaron. "And there was no water for the congregation: and they gathered themselves together against Moses and against Aaron" (Numbers 20:2). But notice, "they gathered themselves together against Moses and against Aaron." Then they once again begin to complain ("chode"). "And the people chode with Moses, and spake, saying, Would God that we had died when our brethren died before the LORD!" (Numbers 20:3). Moses and Aaron immediately took the complaint to God. God answered them. "7. And the LORD spake unto Moses, saying, 8. Take the rod, and gather thou the assembly together, thou, and Aaron thy brother, and speak ye unto the rock before their eyes; and it shall give forth his water, and thou shalt bring forth to them water out of the rock: so thou shalt give the congregation and their beasts drink" (Numbers 20:7–8). They were to take the rod, gather the people, and speak to the rock. Remember, the rock is Christ, and it followed them in the wilderness. "And did all drink the same spiritual drink: for they drank of that spiritual Rock that followed them: and that Rock was Christ" (1 Corinthians 10:4). Then God would give His people water to drink.

Moses and Aaron gathered the people. Moses took the rod, lifted up his hand, and smote the rock twice. Water came out, and the people and their beasts drank. But take notice that Moses did not obey God exactly. What had Moses done wrong? "11. And Moses lifted up his hand, and with his rod he smote the rock twice: and the water came out abundantly, and the congregation drank, and their beasts also. 12. And the LORD spake unto Moses and Aaron, Because ye believed me not, to sanctify me in the eyes of the children of Israel, therefore ye shall not bring this congregation into the land which I have given them" (Numbers 20:11–12). No one else noticed there was a problem. But God spoke to Moses and Aaron and revealed His displeasure. Moses and Aaron would not bring God's people into the Promised Land. Notice that God did not say that they had not believed God. But Moses and Aaron knew. Do you? (God told him to speak to the rock and instead he struck the rock *twice*.) We find that God said Aaron would die because of his disobedience, and his son Eleazar would become the high priest of the people.

Eleazar became the High Priest of the people.

23. And the LORD spake unto Moses and Aaron in mount Hor, by the coast of the land of Edom, saying, 24. Aaron shall be gathered unto his people: for he shall not enter into the land which I have given unto the children of Israel, because ye rebelled against my word at the water of Meribah. 25. Take Aaron and Eleazar his son, and bring them up unto mount Hor: 26. And strip Aaron of his

garments, and put them upon Eleazar his son: and Aaron shall be gathered *unto his people,* and shall die there. 27. And Moses did as the LORD commanded: and they went up into mount Hor in the sight of all the congregation. 28. And Moses stripped Aaron of his garments, and put them upon Eleazar his son; and Aaron died there in the top of the mount: and Moses and Eleazar came down from the mount. 29. And when all the congregation saw that Aaron was dead, they mourned for Aaron thirty days, even all the house of Israel. (Numbers 20:23–29)

Aaron died, and the people mourned him for thirty days.

The journey once again became difficult, and the people's response to that difficulty was to complain. "4. And they journeyed from mount Hor by the way of the Red sea, to compass the land of Edom: and the soul of the people was much discouraged because of the way. 5. And the people spake against God, and against Moses, Wherefore have ye brought us up out of Egypt to die in the wilderness? for *there is* no bread, neither *is there any* water; and our soul loatheth this light bread" (Numbers 21:4–5).

God had delivered them from a land of bondage and provided them with food and water, yet these were their very complaints. They spoke out against God and against Moses. What was God's response this time? "And the LORD sent fiery serpents among the people, and they bit the people; and much people of Israel died" (Numbers 21:6). It wasn't until the fiery serpents were biting them and killing them that they realized that they had sinned against God. They came to Moses, admitted their sin, and asked Moses to pray unto the Lord to take away the serpents. And Moses prayed for the people. God told Moses to make a fiery serpent and put it upon a pole; anyone who would look at it would live. Moses obeyed, and all who looked at that fiery serpent on the pole that had been lifted up did live.

7. Therefore the people came to Moses, and said, We have sinned, for we have spoken against the LORD, and against thee; pray unto the LORD, that he take away the serpents from us. And Moses prayed for the people. 8. And the LORD said unto Moses, Make thee a fiery serpent, and set it upon a pole: and it shall come to pass, that every one that is bitten, when he looketh upon it, shall live. 9. And Moses made a serpent of brass, and put it upon a pole, and it came to pass, that if a serpent had bitten any man, when he beheld the serpent of brass, he lived. (Numbers 21:7–9)

NOTE When Nicodemus came to Jesus by night, Jesus told him how to be saved. Remember that Nicodemus was a Pharisee, which meant he knew the Old Testament history. Jesus took that knowledge and helped him understand what it would take for him to be saved. The people in the wilderness sinned against God when they *rejected* Him and *desired* things God had not given them. They were dying because of their sin. To be saved from death, they had to believe that looking to that serpent on the pole would give them life. It took the same faith as the Israelites had in the wilderness to look at that serpent on the brass pole for Nicodemus to believe that God's only Son, Jesus, would be lifted up. That faith in Him would be the only thing that could save him. "14. And as Moses lifted up the serpent in the wilderness, even so must the Son of man be lifted up: 15. That whosoever believeth in him should not perish, but have eternal life" (John 3:14–15).

LESSON 10 **215** THE BIBLICAL PATH OF LIFE

2. Balaam and His Choice
(Numbers 22–24)

Even without TV, telephones, newspapers, or the Internet, God's people had a reputation. All of the surrounding nations knew this people had a God who delivered them from Egypt—mightily. And along their journey, God had allowed them to defeat enemies—mightily. So when they came to the borders of Moab, the king was afraid. "1. And the children of Israel set forward, and pitched in the plains of Moab on this side Jordan by Jericho. 2. And Balak the son of Zippor saw all that Israel had done to the Amorites. 3. And Moab was sore afraid of the people, because they *were* many: and Moab was distressed because of the children of Israel" (Numbers 22:1–3). King Balak sent word to Balaam to come to him and curse this people, as he thought they were coming to destroy him. The men came to Balaam with "the rewards of divination in their hands." "And the elders of Moab and the elders of Midian departed with the rewards of divination in their hand; and they came unto Balaam, and spake unto him the words of Balak" (Numbers 22:7). If you look at Exodus 23:8, God's people were to take no gift (or bribe) because that gift would "blindeth the wise, and perverteth the words of the righteous." (The lesson we read here of Balaam is a great example as to why God gave us that verse.) He told the men to stay with him, and he would bring them the words that the Lord gave him. "And he said unto them, Lodge here this night, and I will bring you word again, as the LORD shall speak unto me: and the princes of Moab abode with Balaam" (Exodus 22:8).

Balaam's first mistake was to even entertain their request. Read the conversation between God and Balaam. "9. And God came unto Balaam, and said,

THE BIBLICAL PATH OF LIFE 216 LESSON 10

What men *are* these with thee? 10. And Balaam said unto God, Balak the son of Zippor, king of Moab, hath sent unto me, *saying*, 11. Behold, *there is* a people come out of Egypt, which covereth the face of the earth: come now, curse me them; peradventure I shall be able to overcome them, and drive them out. 12. And God said unto Balaam, Thou shalt not go with them; thou shalt not curse the people: for they *are* blessed" (Numbers 22:9–12). God told him not to curse His people, for they were blessed. Balaam obeyed God and sent them away.

But they came back—with a better offer. Not only would he receive the gift they originally offered, but he would also receive great honor and anything else he wanted. "15. And Balak sent yet again princes, more, and more honourable than they. 16. And they came to Balaam, and said to him, Thus saith Balak the son of Zippor, Let nothing, I pray thee, hinder thee from coming unto me: 17. For I will promote thee unto very great honour, and I will do whatsoever thou sayest unto me: come therefore, I pray thee, curse me this people" (Numbers 22:15–17).

Balaam told them no, but once again he invited them to stay the night. "18. And Balaam answered and said unto the servants of Balak, If Balak would give me his house full of silver and gold, I cannot go beyond the word of the LORD my God, to do less or more. 19. Now therefore, I pray you, tarry ye also here this night, that I may know what the LORD will say unto me more" (Numbers 22:18–19). God had already given him His answer. He shouldn't have to repeat Himself. Read Numbers 22:20–35 to recall the events that transpired (his donkey saved his life). Numbers 23

Balak and Balaam.

LESSON 10 **217** THE BIBLICAL PATH OF LIFE

records the blessings Balaam gave to the nation Israel, not the people of Moab. Numbers 24:1 reveals how Balaam saw God react when he obeyed God and blessed God's people instead of cursing them. We see a change in Balaam. He no longer turns "to seek for enchantments, as at other times." The word *enchantments* means "sorcery, indicating some kind of occult practice".

"And when Balaam saw that it pleased the LORD to bless Israel, he went not, as at other times, to seek for enchantments, but he set his face toward the wilderness" (Numbers 24:1). Instead, we see God's Spirit came upon him. This man changed. He blessed Israel greatly, and this angered King Balak. "And Balak's anger was kindled against Balaam, and he smote his hands together: and Balak said unto Balaam, I called thee to curse mine enemies, and, behold, thou hast altogether blessed *them* these three times" (Numbers 24:10). Even with this king's anger, Balaam continued to bless God's people. We see that he went from the present blessings to what God would do in the future. "And now, behold, I go unto my people: come *therefore, and I* will advertise thee what this people shall do to thy people in the latter days" (Numbers 24:14).

Notice that in this, he once again mentioned the promise of God. "I shall see him, but not now: I shall behold him, but not nigh: there shall come a Star out of Jacob, and a Sceptre shall rise out of Israel, and shall smite the corners of Moab, and destroy all the children of Sheth" (Numbers 24:17). Once again, we see the promise of a king from the seed of Jacob—that Star is Jesus (see Luke 1:31–33 and Revelation 22:16).

However, we see the end of Balaam in Numbers 31:8, 16, as he is killed, and we are told the reason why. He could not curse Israel, but he did give counsel to the Midianites on how to defeat the Israelites—send the women to seduce them and bring in idol worship. Satan will work through relationships of the opposite gender to bring ruin to our lives if we are not aware of his devices. We cannot be too careful.

THE BIBLICAL PATH OF LIFE **218** LESSON 10

3. A Disobedient People
(Numbers 25)

When God's people camped near the Moab people, they began to commit adultery with the women of the land (remember they were to be a separate people, and they were not to intermarry with the people of the land). Not only that, but they began to worship their idols; idolatry was equivalent to spiritual adultery. In Numbers 25:3, we see that "the anger of the Lord was kindled against Israel." God commanded that every one who joined in the worship of Baalpeor was to be killed. Remember the first of the Ten Commandments? "3. Thou shalt have no other gods before me. 4. Thou shalt not make unto thee any graven image, or any *likeness of any thing* that *is* in heaven above, or that *is* in the earth beneath, or that *is* in the water under the earth: 5. Thou shalt not bow down thyself to them, nor serve them: for I the LORD thy God *am* a jealous God …" (Exodus 20:3–5a). They broke the law of God they had committed to keep. God punished those who disobeyed. He wanted to eliminate the ones who had left Him and entered into idol worship. They had to be removed to eliminate the spread.

> 1. And Israel abode in Shittim, and the people began to commit whoredom with the daughters of Moab. And they called the people unto the sacrifices of their gods: and the people did eat, and bowed down to their gods. And Israel joined himself unto Baalpeor: and the anger of the LORD was kindled against Israel. And the LORD

LESSON 10 **219** THE BIBLICAL PATH OF LIFE

said unto Moses, Take all the heads of the people, and hang them up before the LORD against the sun, that the fierce anger of the LORD may be turned away from Israel. And Moses said unto the judges of Israel, Slay ye every one his men that were joined unto Baalpeor. (Numbers 25:1–5)

> Slay ye every one his men that were joined unto Baalpeor.

Amazingly, right after this, a man took a Midianitish woman. "And, behold, one of the children of Israel came and brought unto his brethren a Midianitish woman in the sight of Moses, and in the sight of all the congregation of the children of Israel, who *were* weeping *before* the door of the tabernacle of the congregation" (Numbers 25:6). He did it in front of everyone. When Phinehas, the grandson of Aaron, saw this, he took a javelin, entered the tent of this man, and thrust the javelin through both the man and the woman. When he did this, the plague was stayed from the people. We see that twenty-four thousand people died. "7. And when Phinehas, the son of Eleazar, the

THE BIBLICAL PATH OF LIFE **220** LESSON 10

son of Aaron the priest, saw *it*, he rose up from among the congregation, and took a javelin in his hand; 8. And he went after the man of Israel into the tent, and thrust both of them through, the man of Israel, and the woman through her belly. So the plague was stayed from the children of Israel. 9. And those that died in the plague were twenty and four thousand" (Numbers 25:7–9).

Phinehas took a javelin and went into the tent.

Because Phinehas was zealous (jealous with God's jealousy) for God, and he rejected this man who had rejected God and His law, God blessed Phinehas.

10. And the LORD spake unto Moses, saying, 11. Phinehas, the son of Eleazar, the son of Aaron the priest, hath turned my wrath away from the children of Israel, while he was zealous for my sake among them, that I consumed not the children of Israel in my jealousy. 12. Wherefore say, Behold, I give unto him my covenant of peace: And he shall have it, and his seed after him, even the covenant of an everlasting priesthood; because he was zealous for his God, and made an atonement for the children of Israel. (Numbers 25:10–13)

4. Final Provisions before Entering the Promised Land

(Numbers 26–36)

Even through all the troubles and instances of disobedience, we never see God turn from or reject His people. He stayed with them and prepared them to enter the land of promise. Beginning in Numbers 26, we see the second numbering of the people in this book. The old generation had died (the ones who had disobeyed God's command to take the Promised Land), and the new generation was to be prepared to take the Promised Land. Remember that everyone had to die but Caleb and Joshua. They were the only two who were allowed to enter the Promised Land.

> 63. These *are* they that were numbered by Moses and Eleazar the priest, who numbered the children of Israel in the plains of Moab by Jordan *near* Jericho. 64. But among these there was not a man of them whom Moses and Aaron the priest numbered, when they numbered the children of Israel in the wilderness of Sinai. 65. For the LORD had said of them, They shall surely die in the wilderness. And there was not left a man of them, save Caleb the son of Jephunneh, and Joshua the son of Nun. (Numbers 26:63–65)

God promised Moses that he would see the Promised Land, though he would never enter because of his disobedience. "12. And the LORD said unto

THE BIBLICAL PATH OF LIFE 222 LESSON 10

Moses, Get thee up into this mount Abarim, and see the land which I have given unto the children of Israel. 13. And when thou hast seen it, thou also shalt be gathered unto thy people, as Aaron thy brother was gathered. 14. For ye rebelled against my commandment in the desert of Zin, in the strife of the congregation, to sanctify me at the water before their eyes: that is the water of Meribah in Kadesh in the wilderness of Zin" (Numbers 27:12–14).

Joshua was charged before the people.

Moses asked God to appoint a leader for the people after he was gone. "15. And Moses spake unto the LORD, saying, 16. Let the LORD, the God of the spirits of all flesh, set a man over the congregation, 17. Which may go out before them, and which may go in before them, and which may lead them out, and which may bring them in; that the congregation of the LORD be not as sheep which have no shepherd" (Numbers 27:15–17). God appointed Joshua. Joshua was charged before the people.

18. And the LORD said unto Moses, Take thee Joshua the son of Nun, a man in whom *is* the spirit, and lay thine hand upon him; 19. And set him before Eleazar the priest,

Eleazar the high priest.

and before all the congregation; and give him a charge in their sight. 20. And thou shalt put *some* of thine honour upon him, that all the congregation of the children of Israel may be obedient. 21. And he shall stand before Eleazar the priest, who shall ask *counsel* for him after the judgment of Urim before the LORD: at his word shall they go out, and at his word they shall come in, *both* he, and all the children of Israel with him, even all the congregation. 22. And Moses did as the LORD commanded him: and he took Joshua, and set him before Eleazar the priest, and before all the congregation: 23. And he laid his hands upon him, and gave him a charge, as the LORD commanded by the hand of Moses. (Numbers 27:18–23)

The people would lose Moses as their leader, but they would gain Joshua. God had a promise for His people that they would take the land, but that promise came with a warning.

THE BIBLICAL PATH OF LIFE 224 LESSON 10

50. And the LORD spake unto Moses in the plains of Moab by Jordan *near* Jericho, saying, 51. Speak unto the children of Israel, and say unto them, When ye are passed over Jordan into the land of Canaan; 52. Then ye shall drive out all *the inhabitants* of the land from before you, and destroy all their pictures, and destroy all their molten images, and quite pluck down all their high places: 53. And ye shall dispossess the inhabitants of the land, and dwell therein: for I have given you the land to possess it. 54. And ye shall divide the land by lot for an inheritance among your families: *and* to the more ye shall give the more inheritance, and to the fewer ye shall give the less *inheritance:* every man's inheritance shall be in the place where his lot falleth; according to the tribes of your fathers ye shall inherit. 55. But if ye will not drive out the inhabitants of the land from before you; then it shall come to pass, that those which ye let remain of them *shall be* pricks in your eyes, and thorns in your sides, and shall vex you in the land wherein ye dwell. 56. Moreover it shall come to pass, *that* I shall do unto you, as I thought to do unto them. (Numbers 33:50–56)

They must drive **everyone** out of the land. Then they **must** destroy every picture and molten image and pluck down all of their high places (set up for the worship of idols). If they didn't, the people would give them trouble (Numbers 33:55), and God would do to His people what He would have done to the heathen (Numbers 33:56).

LESSON 10 **225** THE BIBLICAL PATH OF LIFE

Numbers 20 – 36 at a Glance:

- **Chapter 20:** Miriam & Aaron died (1, 28), Moses smote and spoke to rock (2-11), Moses can't enter land (12-13)
- **Chapter 21:** Fiery serpents (4-9), traveling (10-20), battle with Amorites (21-32), battle at Edrei (33-35)
- **Chapter 22:** Pitched in plains of Moab and Balaam's donkey speaks
- **Chapter 23:** Balaam's prophecies
- **Chapter 24:** Balaam blesses Israel – promise of Jesus (vs. 17)
- **Chapter 25:** People worshiped idols in Shittim – all were killed (1-5), Phinehas speared man and Midianite woman (6-9) and plagued stayed (after 24,000 killed), Phinehas blessed (10-18)
- **Chapter 26:** Sons 20 & up numbered & land to be divided (52-56), no one left from before but Caleb and Joshua (63-65)
- **Chapter 27:** Laws of inheritance (1-11), Moses sees land from mount (12-14), God chooses Joshua & his charge (15-21)
- **Chapter 28:** Moses tells new generation the laws of sacrifices
- **Chapter 29:** Moses continues with the offerings and Feasts
- **Chapter 30:** Laws concerning vows (especially verse 2)
- **Chapter 31:** Avenge Israelites against Midian
- **Chapter 32:** Inheritance of Rueben and Gad with the promised the will help conquer the land (23)
- **Chapter 33:** Remembering the wilderness journey (1-49), promise of conquest with a warning (50-56)
- **Chapter 34:** Boundaries of Canaan
- **Chapter 35:** Land for Levites (1-8), laws concerning murder and City of Refuge (9-34)
- **Chapter 36:** Laws of female inheritance

THE BIBLICAL PATH OF LIFE 226 LESSON 10

Reinforcement:

Today we saw that the chastisement on the old generation continued, and the new generation prepared to enter the land. We also looked at many opportunities to obey God, and we saw the chastisement when the people disobeyed.

Take a few minutes to brainstorm. Think of different ways we can stop the spiritual adultery we see each day (short of taking a javelin and thrusting someone through!). At the very least, recognize instances of spiritual adultery (e.g., putting events more important than church attendance, putting things or people as more important than God, failing to have a quiet time of prayer and reading God's Word).

Closing:

It would be good to close with a short prayer reinforcing today's lesson. Always include any prayer requests you may have. *Today, pray for God to help us remember that as God's people, we have a reputation to uphold. Help us keep God and His commands as most important in our lives so we can fulfill the duty God requires of us as Christians.*

LESSON 10

Numbers 20–36:
The Next Generation

Read Numbers 20–36. Complete the following.

1. What did the people do once again? (Numbers 20:3) _____ _____ _____ What was Moses' and Aaron's responses? (Numbers 20:6) _____

2. What did God tell Moses to do? (Numbers 20:8) _____ _____ Did he obey? (Numbers 20:11) ____ How did he not obey? _____ _____ What did God tell Moses? (Numbers 20:12) _____ _____ What happened to Aaron? (Numbers 20:28) _____ _____

According to 1 Corinthians 10:4, the Rock is Christ.
He followed them in the wilderness.

3. The people journeyed again, and what did they do again? (Numbers 21:5) _____ What did God send? (Numbers

THE BIBLICAL PATH OF LIFE 228 LESSON 10

21:6)_____ What happened to the

people? _____ What did the people recognize?

(Numbers 21:7a)_____

_____ What did they ask Moses to do? (Numbers 7b)

What did God tell Moses to do? (Numbers 21:8)_____ What

happened? (Numbers 21:9) _____

4. Balak, king of Moab, was afraid of God's people. What did he call Balaam

to do? (Numbers 22:5–6) _____ Balaam went to

God. What did God say? (Numbers 22:12) _____

_____

5. What did Balaam tell the men? (Numbers 22:13) _____

What was Balak's (the king's) response? (Numbers 22:15, 17)_____

_____What did Balaam say? (Numbers 22:18)

_____ What mistake did Balaam make?

(Numbers 22:19) _____ What did God tell

him? (Numbers 22:20–22)_____

_____ Did God really want him to go with

those men? _____ Did Balaam go? _____

6. Read Numbers 22:20–35. Who saved Balaam's life? _____

Who was standing in front of him with a sword? _____

What did Balaam recognize? (Numbers 22:34)_____

What did God's angel tell him to do? (Numbers 22:35) _____

_____Balaam's heart changed. He obeyed God

and blessed God's people.

LESSON 10 **229** THE BIBLICAL PATH OF LIFE

7. What happened again in Numbers 26:2? _____ _____ Who were the only two to enter the Promised Land? (Numbers 26:65) _____ and _____ Who did God appoint as the new leader? (Numbers 18–21) _____

8. What were the people to do upon entering the land? (Numbers 33:52)
_____
_____

Answers:
1. The people complained again; fell upon their faces before the Lord
2. Take the rod and speak to the rock; no; he struck the rock instead of speaking to it; because they didn't believe God, they would not bring the people into the land God gave them; Aaron died
3. Spoke against God and Moses; fiery serpents; those bitten died; they had sinned; pray the Lord would take away the serpents; make a fiery serpent and set it upon a pole; everyone that was bitten, and looked upon the fiery serpent on the pole shall live
4. Curse God's people; he was not to go with them, he was not to curse God's people
5. Go back to your land, God won't let me go; sent more men with promises of promotion and great honor; "if Balak gave me his house full of gold or silver, I cannot go beyond the word of the Lord"; he asked them to stay so that he would know what else the Lord may say to him; God told Balaam to go, but only say God's words
6. Donkey; the angel of the Lord, he had sinned; go with the men, but only speak God's words
7. Moses numbered the people again; Joshua; Caleb; Joshua
8. Drive out all the inhabitants of the land, destroy all their pictures, destroy all their molten images, and pluck down all their high places

THE BIBLICAL PATH OF LIFE **230** LESSON 10

DEUTERONOMY 1–11
REMEMBERING THE PAST AND REVIEWING GOD'S LAWS

LESSON 11

Key Verse

And thou shalt love the LORD thy God with all thine heart, and with all thy soul, and with all thy might.

—DEUTERONOMY 6:5

Key Verse Thought: Read the key verse. Understand that we are to love God with all of our hearts, souls, and might. Realize that the way we show God we love Him is to obey Him in every area of our lives. (See what Jesus said in John 14:15: "If ye love me, keep my commandments.")

Emphasis: Show God we love Him with all of our hearts, souls, and might by our obedience to Him.

Lesson Summary: The book of Deuteronomy begins where Numbers ends. The forty-year journey, which should have taken only a few days, was over, and only three of the original Hebrews numbered in the first census (twenty years old and older) were still alive: Joshua, Caleb, and Moses. What God wanted most from His people was for them to love Him with all of their hearts, souls, and might. If they would have done that, they would not have had to be constantly reminded to obey God and His laws. They would have shown their love for Him by their remembrance of all He had done for them and by their obedience to His Word. In the book of Deuteronomy, God reminds this new generation who He is. He reminds them of the promises and the deliverance He showed their fathers. He continues by reminding them what He expects from them. And most important, they are to teach these things to their children.

The entire book shows the faithfulness of God and reveals that God loves His people.

Suggested Bible Reading to Prepare for This Lesson

- Monday: **Deuteronomy 1–2**
- Tuesday: **Deuteronomy 3–4**
- Wednesday: **Deuteronomy 5–6**
- Thursday: **Deuteronomy 7–8**
- Friday: **Deuteronomy 9–10**
- Saturday: **Deuteronomy 11**

Deuteronomy 1–11
Remembering the Past and Reviewing God's Laws

1 Remember God's Faithfulness (Deuteronomy 1–3)

- God fulfilled his promise to Abraham (Deuteronomy 1:8, 10–11)
- God gave them the land (Deuteronomy 1:21)
- God delivered them from the hand of their enemies in the wilderness (Deuteronomy 1–3:20)
- God would take Moses but give Joshua (Deuteronomy 3:21–28)

2 Remember God's Law (Deuteronomy 4–6)

- Remember the people who turned to Baalpeor? (Deuteronomy 4:3)
- Warning against idolatry (Deuteronomy 4:14–24)
- The Ten Commandments (Deuteronomy 5)
- Remember God's commands and teach them to their children (Deuteronomy 6)

3 Remember God (Deuteronomy 7–11)

- God's chosen people—obey (Deuteronomy 7:6–26)
- God's provision (Deuteronomy 8)
- God's patience with a stiff-necked people (Deuteronomy 9–10)
- God's blessings and curse (Deuteronomy 11)

1. Remember God's Faithfulness
(Deuteronomy 1–3)

God let Joshua know that He would fight for them

This generation had not seen God's deliverance from the land of Egypt. They had to be reminded of that deliverance. They also had to be reminded of the promises God made to these, His people. "8. Behold, I have set the land before you: go in and possess the land which the LORD sware unto your fathers, Abraham, Isaac, and Jacob, to give unto them and to their seed after them. …10. The LORD your God hath multiplied you, and, behold, ye *are* this day as the stars of heaven for multitude" (Deuteronomy 1:8, 10). He reminded them that this was the land he had given them. "Behold, the LORD thy God hath set the land before thee: go up *and* possess *it,* as the LORD God of thy fathers hath said unto thee; fear not, neither be discouraged" (Deuteronomy 1:21). Deuteronomy 1–3:20 is just a reminder of God's constant deliverance during

THE BIBLICAL PATH OF LIFE 236 LESSON 11

the forty years of wandering in the wilderness. We then see God encouraging Joshua with all of this information. "21. And I commanded Joshua at that time, saying, Thine eyes have seen all that the LORD your God hath done unto these two kings: so shall the LORD do unto all the kingdoms whither thou passest. 22. Ye shall not fear them: for the LORD your God he shall fight for you" (Deuteronomy 3:21–22). God let Joshua know that He would fight for them.

NOTE God encouraged Joshua, letting him know that He would be with him and fight for him. Remember that Joshua had been faithful to God and His Word. He had seen God deliver His people and trusted that God would continue to deliver them. He had faith in God. We need to remember that when God places a task before us, He will help us to do it. We just need to remember God and His faithfulness. "Those things, which ye have both learned, and received, and heard, and seen in me, do: and the God of peace shall be with you" (Philippians 4:9).

LESSON 11   THE BIBLICAL PATH OF LIFE

2. Remember God's Law
(Deuteronomy 4–6)

Do you remember the people who turned to Baalpeor? (See Numbers 25.) God utterly destroyed everyone who turned to idols. He wanted any traces of idol worship removed from His people. He told them to remember that God is a jealous God. He would not allow anything (or anyone) to be placed above Him. Read Deuteronomy 4:14–24 and understand what idols are (or can be).

God reminded them that He chose them, and He would be with them. "And because he loved thy fathers, therefore he chose their seed after them, and brought thee out in his sight with his mighty power out of Egypt" (Deuteronomy 4:37).

The old generation had died so God gave this new generation the Ten Commandments (Deuteronomy 5:1–33). (The word *Deuteronomy* means "the second giving of the law.") They were then encouraged to do something extremely important: teach these commandments and all of the statutes of God to their children. "Now these *are* the, the statutes, and the judgments, which the LORD your God commanded to teach you, that ye might do *them* in the land whither ye go to possess it" (Deuteronomy 6:1). The following words in Deuteronomy 6 were extremely important; they were not only to *do them*, but they were to preserve them by teaching them to their children. "6. And these words, which I command thee this day, shall be in thine heart: 7. And thou shalt teach them diligently unto thy children, and shalt talk of them when thou sittest in thine house, and when thou walkest by the way, and when thou liest down, and when thou risest up" (Deuteronomy 6:6–7).

Notice they were to hide God's Word in their hearts (Deuteronomy 6:6) and diligently teach them to their children (Deuteronomy 6:7). They were also to fear God and serve Him. "Thou shalt fear the LORD thy God, and serve him, and shalt swear by his name" (Deuteronomy 6:13). Notice also that Jesus quoted Deuteronomy 6:13, Deuteronomy 6:16 ("Ye shall not tempt the LORD your God, as ye tempted *him* in Massah"), and Deuteronomy 8:3b ("… that man doth not live by bread only, but by every word that proceedeth out of the mouth of the LORD doth man live"), when He was tempted in Matthew 4.

We should read and know Deuteronomy 6 to remind us what we should do, even today.

NOTE It is not enough to know what the Ten Commandments are or even what the rest of the Law says. We must know what God's Word is and do it.

22. But be ye doers of the word, and not hearers only, deceiving your own selves. 23. For if any be a hearer of the word, and not a doer, he is like unto a man beholding his natural face in a glass: 24. For he beholdeth himself, and goeth his way, and straightway forgetteth what manner of man he was. 25. But whoso looketh into the perfect law of liberty, and continueth therein, he being not a forgetful hearer, but a doer of the work, this man shall be blessed in his deed. (James 1:22–25)

If we do what God's Word says, we will be blessed.

3. Remember God
(Deuteronomy 7–11)

They were to remain a separate people unto God. "Neither shalt thou make marriages with them; thy daughter thou shalt not give unto his son, nor his daughter shalt thou take unto thy son" (Deuteronomy 7:3). God had chosen them, not because they were anything special but because God loved them by His grace.

> 6. For thou *art* an holy people unto the LORD thy God: the LORD thy God hath chosen thee to be a special people unto himself, above all people that *are* upon the face of the earth. 7. The LORD did not set his love upon you, nor choose you, because ye *were* more in number than any people; for ye were the fewest of all people: 8. But because the LORD loved you, and because he would keep the oath which he had sworn unto your fathers, hath the LORD brought you out with a mighty hand, and redeemed you out of the house of bondmen, from the hand of Pharaoh king of Egypt. (Deuteronomy 7:6–8)

Deuteronomy 7 continues with blessings for those who obey God.

God told the people to remember Him and the ways He had provided for them during the forty years of wandering (read Deuteronomy 8:1–18). Even through all of the warnings to obey God's commands and to follow God, He knew His people. So He warned them: if they forgot God and worshipped and served other gods, they would perish. "19. And it shall be, if thou do at all forget the LORD thy God, and walk after other gods, and serve them, and worship them, I testify against you this day that ye shall surely perish. 20. As the nations which the LORD destroyeth before your face, so shall ye perish; because ye would not be obedient unto the voice of the LORD your God" (Deuteronomy 8:19–20).

God knew the Israelites would think that they were a really great people to be able to go in and conquer a land with giants, so He warned them about their pride. They were to remember that God chose them, and it wasn't because they were a righteous people. They were taking the land and destroying (and driving out) the wicked because they were a wicked people.

3. Understand therefore this day, that the LORD thy God *is* he which goeth over before thee; *as* a consuming fire he shall destroy them, and he shall bring them down before thy face: so shalt thou drive them out, and destroy them quickly, as the LORD hath said unto thee. 4. Speak not thou in thine heart, after that the LORD thy God hath cast them out from before thee, saying, For my righteousness the LORD hath brought me in to possess this land: but for the wickedness of these nations the LORD doth drive them out from before thee. 5. Not for thy righteousness, or for the uprightness of thine heart, dost thou go to possess their land: but for the wickedness of these nations the LORD thy God doth drive

Israelites gathering Manna.

LESSON 11 **241** THE BIBLICAL PATH OF LIFE

them out from before thee, and that he may perform the word which the LORD sware unto thy fathers, Abraham, Isaac, and Jacob. 6. Understand therefore, that the LORD thy God giveth thee not this good land to possess it for thy righteousness; for thou art a stiffnecked people. (Deuteronomy 9:3–6)

Remember their failures in the past (they had not remained faithful to God; Deuteronomy 9:7–29). If Moses had not repeatedly interceded on the people's behalf, God would have destroyed them long ago. But Moses reminded God of His promise to Abraham, Isaac, and Jacob. "27. Remember thy servants, Abraham, Isaac, and Jacob; look not unto the stubbornness of this people, nor to their wickedness, nor to their sin: … 29. Yet they *are* thy people and thine inheritance, which thou broughtest out by thy mighty power and by thy stretched out arm" (Deuteronomy 9:27, 29). God is always faithful to His Word.

In Deuteronomy 10, God reminded them of the two stone tables Moses made with the Ten Commandments. He once again told them what He required of them. "12. And now, Israel, what doth the LORD thy God require of thee, but to fear the LORD thy God, to walk in all his ways, and to love him, and to serve the LORD thy God with all thy heart and with all thy soul, 13. To keep the commandments of the LORD, and his statutes, which I command thee this day for thy good?" (Deuteronomy 10:12–13).

Read what Jesus said: "21. He that hath my commandments, and keepeth them, he it is that loveth me: and he that loveth me shall be loved of my Father, and I will love him, and will manifest myself to him. … 23. Jesus answered and said unto him, If a man love me, he will keep my words: and my Father will love him, and we will come unto him, and make our abode with him" (John 14:21, 23).

Deuteronomy 11 tells of God's blessings to those who obey Him and the curse upon those who do not obey Him. Obedience is very important to God.

THE BIBLICAL PATH OF LIFE 242 LESSON 11

NOTE They were to remain a separate people unto God (Deuteronomy 7:3). He did not want His people to intermarry with the idolatrous nations that lived in the land they were preparing to enter. God does not want His people to marry people who are "lost" today (those who do not belong to Jesus). "Be ye not unequally yoked together with unbelievers: for what fellowship hath righteousness with unrighteousness? and what communion hath light with darkness?" (2 Corinthians 6:14). God wanted His people (and Christians today) to remain faithful to Him.

Reinforcement:

God wants us to remember all the good things He has done for us, not because we are good or deserve it but because He is good and faithful to His Word. He expects obedience from us because of the grace He has shown us. We show God we love Him by our obedience to Him. And we are to love Him with all of our hearts, souls, and might.

Closing:

It would be good to close with a short prayer reinforcing today's lesson. Always include any prayer requests you may have. *Today, pray for God to help us to remember Him. Help us to love Him with all of our hearts, souls, and might, especially to show we love Him with our obedience to Him.*

LESSON 11

Deuteronomy 1–11:
Remembering the Past and Reviewing God's Laws

Read Deuteronomy 1–11. Complete the following.

1. What happened to everyone over the age of twenty (except for Joshua and Caleb and Moses at this point?) _____ _____ Why? _____ _____

Note: Because the old generation had died, God had to remind the new generation of his promises.

2. How long had the people been wandering in the wilderness? (Deuteronomy 1:3) _____ What did God tell His people, and to whom was it promised? (Deuteronomy 1:8) _____ What was the other part of the promise? (Deuteronomy 1:10) _____ _____ Had it come true? _____

3. Who would lead the people into the land? (Deuteronomy 1:38) _____ What would God do? (Deuteronomy 1:30) _____ _____ _____

THE BIBLICAL PATH OF LIFE 244 LESSON 11

4. Remember what happened at Baalpeor (in Numbers 25). Why had God repeatedly told His people not to worship idols? (Deuteronomy 4:24) _____ _____ But of what does God remind them? (Deuteronomy 4:37) _____

_____

5. Because the old generation had died, of what does God remind the new generation? (Deuteronomy 5:1–33) _____

_____

This is the second giving of the Law.

6. What were they to do? (Deuteronomy 6:1) _____ and in Deuteronomy 6:7: _____ Where were they to put God's words? (Deuteronomy 6:6) _____ What does it say in Psalm 119:11? _____ Why should we hide God's Word in our hearts? _____

Notice that Jesus quoted the Bible when Satan tempted Him.
We should know it for the same reason.

7. What did God tell them in Deuteronomy 7:3? _____ _____ Why not? (Deuteronomy 7:4, 6–8) _____

_____

_____

LESSON 11 **245** THE BIBLICAL PATH OF LIFE

8. With whom will God keep his covenant? (Deuteronomy 7:9) _____

_____ How long? _____

_____

9. What if they forgot God and worshipped and served other gods? (Deuteronomy 8:19–20) _____

_____ Why? _____

_____

10. Why was God going to drive out the inhabitants of the land? (Deuteronomy 9:4b) _____ Were the Israelites a great people? (Deuteronomy 9:4–7) _____ What did God call them? _____ What does it say in Proverbs 16:18? Do you understand why God warned them about pride? _____

11. Where were the stone tables of the Law to be kept? (Deuteronomy 10:2–5) _____

12. What does God once again tell the people that He required of them? (Deuteronomy 10:12–13) _____

_____

_____

(Also remember John 14:21, 23.)

THE BIBLICAL PATH OF LIFE 246 LESSON 11

Answers:

1. They died; they disobeyed God and did not get to enter the Promised Land

2. Forty years; go in and possess the land God promised to Abraham, Isaac, and Jacob; they were as the stars of heave for multitude; yes

3. Joshua; God would go before them and fight for them

4. God is a consuming fire, a jealous God; God loved their fathers and chose their seed after them

5. The Ten Commandments (or God's Law)

6. Know and do God's commands; teach God's Word diligently to their children; in their hearts; hide God's Word in our hearts; so we don't sin against God

7. Do not marry the people of the land; the people of the land would turn their hearts away from God and they are to be a holy people to the Lord, for he had chosen them to be his special people

8. With those who love God and keep His commandments; to a thousand generations

9. They would surely perish; because they would not be obedient to the voice of God

10. For the wickedness of these nations; no; a stiffnecked people; pride goes before destruction, and a haughty spirit before a fall; yes

11. Ark of the covenant

12. To fear God, to walk in all his ways, to love him, to serve God with all your heart and soul, to keep the commandments of the Lord, and his statutes

LESSON 11 **247** THE BIBLICAL PATH OF LIFE

DEUTERONOMY 12–34
PLANNING THE TRIP INTO THE PROMISED LAND

LESSON 12

Key Verse

Be strong and of a good courage, fear not, nor be afraid of them: for the LORD thy God, he it is that doth go with thee; he will not fail thee, nor forsake thee.

—DEUTERONOMY 31:6

Key Verse Thought: Read the key verse. Remember that God's people were preparing to go into the land of promise to conquer it. They had heard the stories of giants in the land, yet they got ready to enter. God wanted to encourage and reassure them. Think of a time you truly have been afraid. The one time you never have to be afraid is when you do something that God has told you to do. God told His people to go and possess the Promised Land. They were not to be afraid. God would be with them, and He would not fail them or leave them. God will do the same for us today, if we will walk with Him.

Emphasis: God wanted His people to know that He would be with them wherever He led them. The constant theme we have seen is the

THE BIBLICAL PATH OF LIFE **248** LESSON 11

importance of obedience to God. He wanted obedience from His people, but He gave them the choice.

Lesson Summary: In the previous lesson in the study of Deuteronomy, we looked back to what God had done for His people (Deuteronomy 1–11). This week, the rest of the book looks forward to the future (Deuteronomy 12–34).

Deuteronomy reminds us of the Law as the people are brought to the brink of the Promised Land, ready to take possession. All of Israel gathered together. Moses warned the people not to forget the words of God's law. He detailed specific requirements of the Law that would establish them and prepare them to have a kingdom ruled by God, giving special attention to the idolatry they would have to deal with once in the Promised Land. Moses then laid out before the people the blessings for following God's law and warned them of the curse of God if they failed to obey His law. The constant theme is the importance of obedience to God. He wanted obedience from His people, but He gave them the choice.

Joshua was appointed the new leader (Deuteronomy 31). Moses gave his blessing and then died (Deuteronomy 33–34).

Suggested Bible Reading to Prepare for This Lesson

⊘ Mon: **Deuteronomy 12–15**   ⊘ Thu: **Deuteronomy 24-27**

⊘ Tue: **Deuteronomy 16–19**   ⊘ Fri: **Deuteronomy 28-31**

⊘ Wed: **Deuteronomy 20–23**   ⊘ Sat: **Deuteronomy 32–34**

LESSON 11 249 THE BIBLICAL PATH OF LIFE

Deuteronomy 12–34
Planning the Trip into the Promised Land

1 Know Their Heritage (Deuteronomy 12–29)

- How to take the land (Deuteronomy 12–13)
- Remember the laws of God (Deuteronomy 14–26)
- Blessings of obedience and curses for disobedience (Deuteronomy 27–28)
- A renewed covenant (Deuteronomy 29)

2 Moses Will Pass, but God Provides Joshua (Deuteronomy 30–34)

- Moses encourages the people to live for God (Deuteronomy 30)
- Joshua appointed as new leader (Deuteronomy 31:1–8)
- Moses takes written law; gives it to the Levites (Deuteronomy 31:9–26)
- The song of Moses and his death (Deuteronomy 31:27–34:12)

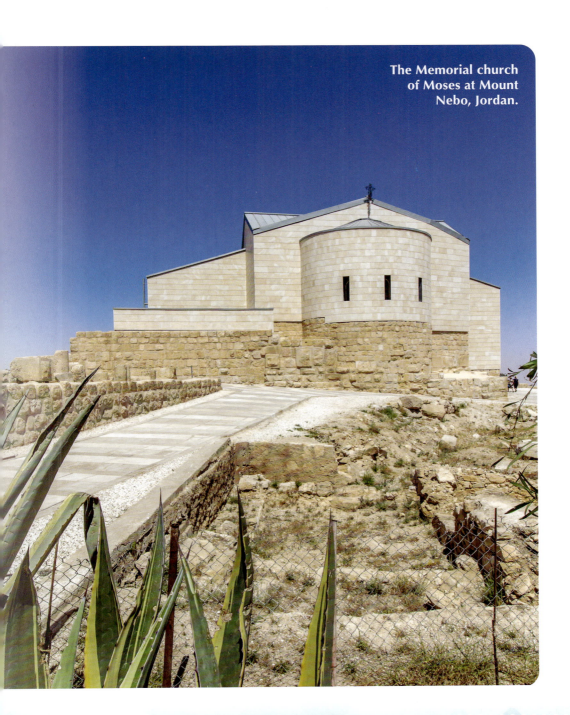

The Memorial church of Moses at Mount Nebo, Jordan.

LESSON 12   **251**   THE BIBLICAL PATH OF LIFE

1. Know Their Heritage
(Deuteronomy 12–29)

These eighteen chapters tell what they were to do to take the land of Canaan and make it the land of Israel. First and foremost, they were to utterly destroy any evidence of idol worship. Then they were to establish one place to worship God (Deuteronomy 12). They were warned not to listen to false prophets (Deuteronomy 13).

"15. The LORD thy God will raise up unto thee a Prophet from the midst of thee, of thy brethren, like unto me; unto him ye shall hearken; … 18. I will raise them up a Prophet from among their brethren, like unto thee, and will put my words in his mouth; and he shall speak unto them all that I shall command him. 19. And it shall come to pass, *that* whosoever will not hearken unto my words which he shall speak in my name, I will require *it* of him" (Deuteronomy 18:15, 18–19). Once again, we see the promise of Jesus. He was the "Prophet" who would come from this people. They were to hear Him. Compare these verses to the following from Acts:

> 22. For Moses truly said unto the fathers, A prophet shall the Lord your God raise up unto you of your brethren, like unto me; him shall ye hear in all things whatsoever he shall say unto you. 23. And it shall come to pass, *that* every soul, which will not hear that prophet, shall be destroyed from among the people. 24. Yea, and all the prophets from Samuel and those that follow after, as many as have spoken, have likewise foretold of these days. 25. Ye are the

THE BIBLICAL PATH OF LIFE **252** LESSON 12

children of the prophets, and of the covenant which God made with our fathers, saying unto Abraham, And in thy seed shall all the kindreds of the earth be blessed. 26. Unto you first God, having raised up his Son Jesus, sent him to bless you, in turning away every one of you from his iniquities. (Acts 3:22–26)

Archaeological site of Mount Gerzim.

Moses then reminded this new generation of the laws God gave to His people that they might be pleasing to Him and blessed in the land (Deuteronomy 14–26:15). Finally, they were reminded that they were to "… walk in his ways, and keep his statutes, and his commandments, and his judgments, and to hearken unto his voice" (Deuteronomy 26:17). God reminded them that they were to be His "peculiar people." "And the LORD hath avouched thee this day to be his peculiar people, as he hath promised thee, and that *thou* shouldest keep all his commandments" (Deuteronomy 26:18). Moses then had some of the people stand on Mount Gerzim to bless the people and had the others stand on Mount Ebal to curse. The people proceeded to shout from the mount the things that God would curse (Deuteronomy 27:11–26). The blessings of obedience came next (Deuteronomy 28:1–14). After this, God warned of the punishment for anyone

LESSON 12   THE BIBLICAL PATH OF LIFE

who disobeyed (Deuteronomy 28:15–68). No one could say they did not know what God would bless and what God would curse. Moses encouraged them to obey. God renewed His covenant with His people before they entered into the land. That covenant came with a warning (Deuteronomy 29:18–29) to all of those who turned their hearts away from God.

Today, it is very important that each person be grounded in the principles in God's Word. It is imperative for each person to know what he or she believes. Part of the reason we go to Sunday School and have Bible studies is to dig deeper into what God's Word says. It allows us to ask questions, to discuss, and to better understand what it says in the Bible. If we are doing our job, we not only are learning what the Bible says, but we are comparing scripture to scripture, helping us to better understand it as a whole. Moses was trying to help the people understand the very basics of God's Word before they entered into a pagan land. The land was full of idol worship. The people of the land did not worship the true God. God's people were to hear, know, and be grounded in what God's Word was, or they could never conquer and possess the land as God required them to do. Before Moses retold them the laws of God, he gave them a warning: "Ye shall not do after all *the things* that we do here this day, every man whatsoever *is* right in his own eyes" (Deuteronomy 12:8). If only they had listened to God's Word and heeded what was therein! We will see that by the time Judges comes around, this is the very condition of God's people.

We must know God's Word and help our children and grandchildren to have a desire to know His Word, or they will live in this world in the very same condition the Israelites lived in the land of promise, doing whatever is right in their own eyes. That has quickly become the condition of the world we live in today. We must do our best to live in obedience to God and to reach our kids so they can make a difference, or we will not only fail to improve the conditions of the life we are living, but we will lose our own children.

2. Moses Will Pass, but God Provides Joshua
(Deuteronomy 30–34)

Moses told the people, once again, to obey God. They knew the consequences if they disobeyed, yet they had to constantly be reminded to obey. Moses foresaw the future years and knew they would fail to keep their covenant with God, and punishment would come. But he also saw their restoration and the promises of God fulfilled. Moses made it plain to them. If they obeyed God, they would live. If they choose to disobey, they would die.

15. See, I have set before thee this day life and good, and death and evil; 16. In that I command thee this day to love the LORD thy God, to walk in his ways, and to keep his commandments and his statutes and his judgments, that thou mayest live and multiply: and the LORD thy God shall bless thee in the land whither thou goest to possess it. 17. But if thine heart turn away, so that thou wilt not hear, but shalt be drawn away, and worship other gods, and serve them; 18. I denounce unto you this day, that ye shall surely perish, and that ye shall not prolong your days upon the land, whither thou passest over Jordan to go to possess it. 19. I call heaven and earth to record this day against you, that I have set before you life and death, blessing and cursing: therefore choose life, that both thou

The books of the Law were kept in the ark of the covenant of the Lord.

and thy seed may live: 20. That thou mayest love the LORD thy God, and that thou mayest obey his voice, and that thou mayest cleave unto him: for he is thy life, and the length of thy days: that thou mayest dwell in the land which the LORD sware unto thy fathers, to Abraham, to Isaac, and to Jacob, to give them. (Deuteronomy 30:15–20)

God left the choice in our hands—life or death, blessing or curse—but He asks us to choose life because of His great love for us.

Before Moses introduced Joshua as his successor, he encouraged God's people. "Be strong and of a good courage, fear not, nor be afraid of them: for the LORD thy God, he *it is* that doth go with thee; he will not fail thee, nor forsake thee" (Deuteronomy 31:6). All of these things were written down and given to the Levites to keep so the people would *never* forget. These books of the Law were kept in the ark of the covenant of the Lord. God knew His people. He knew they would turn from Him and be punished. God gave Moses a song to give to the people. It was to be a song of joy. Even though Moses would no longer be with them, they were to know God would be. And He had given them Joshua, who was presented as God's man.

God allowed Moses to see the Promised Land before he died.

48. And the LORD spake unto Moses that selfsame day, saying, 49. Get thee up into this mountain Abarim, *unto* mount Nebo, which

THE BIBLICAL PATH OF LIFE 256 LESSON 12

is in the land of Moab, that *is* over against Jericho; and behold the land of Canaan, which I give unto the children of Israel for a possession: 50. And die in the mount whither thou goest up, and be gathered unto thy people; as Aaron thy brother died in mount Hor, and was gathered unto his people: 51. Because ye trespassed against me among the children of Israel at the waters of Meribah-Kadesh, in the wilderness of Zin; because ye sanctified me not in the midst of the children of Israel. 52. Yet thou shalt see the land before *thee;* but thou shalt not go thither unto the land which I give the children of Israel. (Deuteronomy 32:48–52)

Moses blessed the tribes (Deuteronomy 33) and then went up onto the mountain of Nebo. God showed him the land he would never enter, but God told Moses that this was the land of promise, and He wanted Moses to see it, even though he could not enter. Moses was 120 years old, yet he was not as an old man. "And Moses was an hundred and twenty years old when he died: his eye was not dim, nor his natural force abated" (Deuteronomy 34:7). Moses died there on the mount, and God buried him. "5. So Moses the servant of the LORD died there in the land of Moab, according to the word of the LORD. 6. And he buried him in a valley in the land of Moab, over against Bethpeor: but no man knoweth of his sepulchre unto this day" (Deuteronomy 34:5–6). We get an insight into his death in Jude 1:9, which tells us, "Yet Michael the archangel, when contending with the devil he disputed about the body of Moses, durst not bring against him a railing accusation, but said, The Lord rebuke thee." For some reason (untold in scripture), Satan wanted Moses' body, but since God buried it, Satan could not have it.

Joshua was now the leader of God's people and was ready to lead them into the Promised Land.

LESSON 12 **257** THE BIBLICAL PATH OF LIFE

Reinforcement:

Remember that this was a new generation of people who needed to be reminded of what God's laws were. We should remind ourselves often what God's laws are so that we do not forget to keep them. God wants us to walk in His ways by obeying His commands. He will not fail us or forsake us.

Closing:

It would be good to close with a short prayer reinforcing today's lesson. Always include any prayer requests you may have. *Today, pray for God to help us obey Him. Help us make the right choices that will please God so we can walk with Him in His ways.*

THE BIBLICAL PATH OF LIFE **258** LESSON 12

LESSON 12

Deuteronomy 12–34:
Planning the Trip into the Promised Land

Read Deuteronomy 12–34. Complete the following.

1. What was the first thing God's people were to do when they enter the Promised Land? (Deuteronomy 12:2–3) _____
_____
_____

What does Deuteronomy 12:14 tell them to do? _____
_____
_____

2. What was God's warning for His people? (Deuteronomy 12:8)
_____
_____

3. Moses reminded this new generation of God's laws. What is one in Deuteronomy 14:22? _____
Why did God want that? (Deuteronomy 14:28–29) _____
_____
_____

LESSON 12 259 THE BIBLICAL PATH OF LIFE

4. What does God want His people to do? (Deuteronomy 26:16–17) _____
_____
_____

What are they to be to God? (Deuteronomy 26:18–19) _____
_____

Many laws were repeated for the people to hear so they would not forget to obey God.
Moses had some stand on Mount Gerizim to shout blessings and had others stand on Mount Ebal to shout curses.

5. Which would you rather have: blessings or curses? _____ According to Deuteronomy 28:1–2, how could the people be blessed?
_____
_____
_____ With all of this came a warning (Deuteronomy 28:15). What was it? _____
_____

6. Notice that God placed choices before the people. What were they? (Deuteronomy 30:15) _____
_____ What did God want them to do? (Deuteronomy 30:16) What if they didn't obey? (Deuteronomy 30:17–18) _____
_____ What did God want them to choose? (Deuteronomy 30:19) _____ Do we have a choice to obey God? _____

THE BIBLICAL PATH OF LIFE · LESSON 12

7. What does Deuteronomy 31:6 say? _____

_____ Can you think of any reasons why they may be

afraid? _____

8. What was Moses allowed to see? (Deuteronomy 34:1, 4) _____

_____ What happened in Deuteronomy

34:5? _____ Who buried Moses? (Deuteronomy 34:6) _____

How old was Moses when he died? (Deuteronomy 34:7) _____

Deuteronomy 34:7 tells us that "his eye was not dim, nor his natural force abated."

What do you think that means? _____

_____

9. Who became the leader of God's people after Moses? (Deuteronomy 34:9)

_____

Answers:

1. Utterly destroy all of the places the nations had served their gods; overthrow their altars, break their pillars, burn their groves with fire, hew down the graven images, and destroy the names of them out of that place; over burnt offerings and do as God commands in the place that He chooses

2. Every man is to not do what is right in their own eyes

3. Tithe on the increase of their seed; to take care of the Levites, the stranger, the fatherless, and the widow so they can eat and be satisfied

4. To make Him their God, to walk in His ways, to keep His statutes, His commandments, His judgments, and to listen to His voice; be His peculiar people and a holy people to the Lord

5. Hearken diligently to the voice of the Lord and do all His commands; curses would come upon them and overtake them

6. Life and good, death and evil; love God, walk in His ways, keep His commandments, obey God; surely perish and not prolong their days in the Promised Land; life; yes

7. Be strong and of a good courage, fear not, nor be afraid of them, for God will go with them and not fail or forsake them; battles, giants, etc.

8. The land promised to Abraham, Isaac, and Jacob; Moses died; God; 120 years old; he didn't die of old age, he was still physically strong

9. Joshua

JESUS IN THE OLD TESTAMENT

JESUS FULFILLED THE LAW

LESSON 13

Key Verse

For the law of the Spirit of life in Christ Jesus hath made me free from the law of sin and death. For what the law could not do, in that it was weak through the flesh, God sending his own Son in the likeness of sinful flesh, and for sin, condemned sin in the flesh.

—ROMANS 8:2–3

Key Verse Thought: Read the key verse. Understand that Jesus set us free from the law that condemned us to death because of our sins. We could never fulfill that law, but Jesus did and paid the penalty to save our lives.

Emphasis: In the books of the Law, we saw the importance of recognizing sin and even the cost of sin—the shedding of blood. It was just a *picture* for us to understand of what Jesus one day did on the cross.

Lesson Summary: In this study, we have been learning about the first five books in the Old Testament, the books we call the Law. In those books we watched as God gradually, over time, revealed himself to mankind. He allowed us to see His magnificent holiness—perfect and sinless—and also just how sinful man is. God showed from the beginning that it took the shedding of blood to cover man's sins. At the same time He revealed that He would one day send the perfect *once-and-for-all* sacrifice to take away man's sin. This week as we look in Hebrews 10, we will see that the Law was a picture to help us understand just what it was that Jesus had to fulfill *completely* in order to take away our sins. When we accept the gift God gave us in His Son, Jesus, He then will write His Law on our hearts. We have no excuse. We know. We are to live our lives pleasing God.

Suggested Bible Reading to Prepare for This Lesson

- Monday: **Hebrews 10:1–23**
- Tuesday: **Proverbs 21**
- Wednesday: **Proverbs 22**
- Thursday: **Proverbs 23**
- Friday: **Proverbs 24**
- Saturday: **Hebrews 10:1–23**

LESSON 13 · 263 · THE BIBLICAL PATH OF LIFE

Jesus in the Old Testament
Jesus Fulfilled the Law

1 ## The Shadow: Hebrews 10:1–4

- The Law was a picture.
- The sacrifices were to make us remember.

2 ## The Reality: Hebrews 10:5–8

- Yearly sacrifices would not do.
- Jesus came to do God's will.

3 ## The Grace: Hebrews 10:9–10

- God takes away the old sacrificial system.
- God establishes grace.
- God allows anyone to be sanctified.

4 ## Each Remember: Hebrews 10:16–25

- God places His Law in Christian's hearts.
- Sins are forgiven and forgotten.
- Live faithfully pleasing God.

LESSON 13 | 265 | THE BIBLICAL PATH OF LIFE

1. The Shadow:
Hebrews 10:1–4

In the books of the Law, we saw the importance of recognizing sin and the extreme cost of sin. The sacrificial system that covered our sins for a time was a "shadow of good things to come" (Hebrews 10:1). Those old sacrifices could never take away our sins. "For *it is* not possible that the blood of bulls and of goats should take away sins" (Hebrews 10:4). But it made us *remember* each year the cost of our sins. It cost a life—the shedding of blood. It was a constant reminder that we are sinful. "But in those *sacrifices there is* a remembrance again *made* of sins every year" (Hebrews 10:3). So we see that the Old Testament's sacrificial system was just a *picture* for us to understand what Jesus did for us on the cross. Because it was a picture, it was not the real thing. Jesus was the real, once-and-for-all, perfect sacrifice that took away sin.

The perfect sacrifice that took away sin.

THE BIBLICAL PATH OF LIFE • LESSON 13

2. The Reality:
Hebrews 10:5–8

We see, then, what the yearly sacrifices would not do. "Wherefore when he cometh into the world, he saith, Sacrifice and offering thou wouldest not, but a body hast thou prepared me" (Hebrews 10:5). It would take a perfect man (God's Son) to purchase man's salvation once and for all. Although the Law was impossible for man to fulfill, God provided His Son, Jesus, to fulfill the Law for us. "Then said I, Lo, I come (in the volume of the book it is written of me,) to do thy will, O God" (Hebrews 10:7). So we see that what the Law could not do (make us pure before God), Christ did.

It would take a perfect man to purchase man's salvation.

3. The Grace:
Hebrews 10:9–10

So we understand that God has taken away the Old Testament sacrificial system and replaced it, once and for all, with the blood of Jesus dying on the cross, "Then said he, Lo, I come to do thy will, O God. He taketh away the first, that he may establish the second" (Hebrews 10:9). That is, He replaced the old sacrificial system with the "second," the second being grace. "For the law was given by Moses, *but* grace and truth came by Jesus Christ" (John 1:17). We already looked at the reason for the Law—to show us our sin (remember Romans 3:20—"Therefore by the deeds of the law there shall no flesh be justified in his sight: for by the law is the knowledge of sin"). Even though the Law could not save us, God gives us grace that does. "Moreover the law entered, that the offence might abound. But where sin abounded, grace did much more abound" (Romans 5:20). An important thing to remember is that we do not deserve salvation. Jesus bought it with His life so God could give us salvation as a free gift. "For by grace are ye saved through faith; and that not of yourselves: it is the gift of God" (Ephesians 2:8).

The perfect sacrifice that took away sin.

4. Each Remember:
Hebrews 10:16–23

God expects Christians to know what the Old Testament Law says. Otherwise, Christians would never understand just how sinful they are. But when Jesus died on the cross, we were set free; Christians no longer live under the Law. "For sin shall not have dominion over you: for ye are not under the law, but under grace" (Romans 6:14).

13. For the promise, that he should be the heir of the world, *was* not to Abraham, or to his seed, through the law, but through the righteousness of faith. 14. For if they which are of the law *be* heirs, faith is made void, and the promise made of none effect: 15. Because the law worketh wrath: for where no law is, there *is* no transgression. 16. Therefore it is of faith, that *it might be* by grace; to the end the promise might be sure to all the seed; not to that only which is of the law, but to that also which is of the faith of Abraham; who is the father of us all. (Romans 4:13–16)

When Jesus died on the cross, we were set free.

LESSON 13 **269** THE BIBLICAL PATH OF LIFE

The promise given to Abraham was because of faith, not the Law. It takes faith to accept the grace of God. That guarantees that *anyone* who asks can receive. "For whosoever shall call upon the name of the Lord shall be saved" (Romans 10:13).

God has now written His Law on the Christian's heart and mind. "This *is* the covenant that I will make with them after those days, saith the Lord, I will put my laws into their hearts, and in their minds will I write them" (Hebrews 10:16). His Spirit lives inside each Christian, constantly reminding him or her of God's will. "For they that are after the flesh do mind the things of the flesh; but they that are after the Spirit the things of the Spirit" (Romans 8:5). We must hide God's Word in our hearts so we can live for Him. "Thy word have I hid in mine heart, that I might not sin against thee" (Psalm 119:11).

Because Jesus took away our sins, we can boldly (have freedom to speak all we think, in confidence) enter God's presence. "Having therefore, brethren, boldness to enter into the holiest by the blood of Jesus" (Hebrews 10:19). Christians should live like they belong to God. We should "hold fast the profession of our faith without wavering" (Hebrews 10:23). We can now claim new lives, so we must then live new lives. "Therefore if any man *be* in Christ, *he* is a new creature: old things are passed away; behold,

> We must hide God's Word in our hearts so we can live for Him.

THE BIBLICAL PATH OF LIFE 270 LESSON 13

all things are become new" (2 Corinthians 5:17). We now live new lives of obedience to God and His commands. "And Samuel said, Hath the LORD *as great* delight in burnt offerings and sacrifices, as in obeying the voice of the LORD? Behold, to obey *is* better than sacrifice, *and* to hearken than the fat of rams" (1 Samuel 15:22). *Hearken* means "to listen; to give heed; pay attention." If you remember, Saul did not wait on Samuel to come (as he was told to do). He did not obey. (We will look at this in future lessons.) Instead, he thought it would be better to offer sacrifices to God. God didn't want the sacrifice. He wanted obedience. He doesn't want anything but our obedience. It is better to obey God in the first place than to break His laws. God expects His people to obey Him.

NOTE

The final thought in Hebrews 10:24–25 is as follows: "24. And let us consider one another to provoke unto love and to good works: 25. Not forsaking the assembling of ourselves together, as the manner of some *is*; but exhorting *one another:* and so much the more, as ye see the day approaching." The reality of Christ's sacrifice and God's grace extended to us should constrain us to assemble together even more, encouraging one another to walk worthy of the gift of forgiveness and salvation.

Reinforcement:

Think back on these five books of the Law and the tedious, detailed laws that God instituted, which He expected man to observe. These were given to keep man in constant awareness of how far he had fallen short of God's glory and the terrible price that had to be paid to bring man back into right standing with his Creator. But even through all of these laws and statutes, the blood sacrifices of animals only covered sin until the true sacrifice would come with pure blood that would remove sin. Remember to hide God's Word in your heart, so you won't sin against God. Think often of Christ, broken and bleeding on the cross, being offered as the perfect sacrifice to atone for our sins. You may want to draw a large heart and write some of God's commands on it to remember that we are to write God's Word on our hearts so that we won't sin against Him.

Closing:

It would be good to close with a short prayer reinforcing today's lesson. Always include any prayer requests you may have. *Today, pray for God to help us recognize what Jesus did and to remember to read God's Word daily to hide it in our hearts so we can live lives pleasing to Him.*

THE BIBLICAL PATH OF LIFE

LESSON 13

Jesus in the Old Testament
Jesus Fulfilled the Law

Read Hebrews 10:1–23. Complete the following.

1. According to Hebrews 10:1, what was a shadow of good things to come? _____ What is the meaning of "not the very image"? _____ _____ Could it ever make the "comers" perfect? _____

2. Why did they continually sacrifice in the Old Testament? (Hebrews 10:3) _____

3. What was *not* possible with the Old Testament sacrifices? (Hebrews 10:4) _____ _____

4. In Hebrews 10:5, who is the "he" who "cometh into the world"? _____ He understood what would not do? _____ _____ What did he know God had prepared instead? _____ _____ _____

LESSON 13   273   THE BIBLICAL PATH OF LIFE

5. How do we know Jesus came to do God's will? (Hebrews 10:7) _____

6. Did God take pleasure in the Old Testament sacrificial system? (Hebrews 10:6, 8) _____ What did God take away because of Jesus' doing His will? (Hebrews 10:9) _____ Jesus did that to establish the "second." Write John 1:17 _____
_____

Jesus came to take away the Old Testament sacrificial system and establish grace.

7. Do you remember the purpose of the Law? (Romans 3:20) _____
_____

8. What happened when Jesus offered His body once and for all? (Hebrews 10:10) _____

Sanctified means "to render clean in a moral sense, to purify." Jesus cleansed us.

9. Do we deserve salvation? (Ephesians 2:8) _____
What is it? _____

10. After Jesus offered Himself for our sins, what did He do? (Hebrews 10:12) _____
_____

THE BIBLICAL PATH OF LIFE   274   LESSON 13

11. Now, instead of the stone tablets (God's law that was kept in the ark of the covenant), where is God's law? (Hebrews 10:16) _____ and _____

_____

When someone asks Jesus to forgive him of his sins,
God's Spirit comes and lives in his heart.
We then call that person a Christian (or a believer because
the person believes Jesus died for his sins.)

12. What happens when God's law is written on a believer's heart? (Romans 8:5)

_____

_____

With God's Spirit living in a Christian's heart,
he or she constantly is reminded to obey God.

13. What will help us live for Jesus? (Psalm 119:11) _____

_____

14. Because Jesus took away our sins, what can we now do? (Hebrews 10:19)

_____

Because our sins are forgiven, we can once again
have a personal relationship with God.

15. Write 2 Corinthians 5:17 _____

_____

LESSON 13 **275** THE BIBLICAL PATH OF LIFE

16. Remember that King Saul disobeyed God. What did Samuel tell Saul God wanted? (1 Samuel 15:22) _____

_____

It is better to obey God than to break His laws in the first place.

17. Because of all we have learned today, what should we try to do?

_____

The most important thing we can do as Christians is to obey God

Answers:

1. The law, or sacrificial system that covered our sins for a time; it was a picture, not the real thing; no
2. A remembrance
3. That the blood of bulls and goats should take away sins
4. Jesus; God didn't require continual sacrifice and offerings anymore; Jesus as the perfect sacrifice (a body that was prepared)
5. It was written throughout the Bible
6. No; took away the first; For the law was given by Moses, but grace and truth came by Jesus Christ
7. By the law is the knowledge of sin
8. We can be sanctified
9. No; it is a gift of God
10. Sat down on the right hand of God
11. In our hearts; in our minds
12. They that are after the spirit mind the things of the spirit
13. Hiding God's Word in our hearts
14. Boldness to enter God's presence
15. Therefore if any man be in Christ, he is a new creature: old things are passed away; behold, all things are become new
16. To hearken (to listen, to give heed, or pay attention) to God and obedience is more important to God than a sacrifice
17. Obey God's Word

THE BIBLICAL PATH OF LIFE 276 LESSON 13

www.lighthouse.pub

Visit our website
to purchase books and preview
upcoming titles.

Contact us at:
feedback@lighthouse.pub

Copyright © 2019, w. Lovik
All rights reserved